Dwayne's Guitar Lessons
Presents:

Guitar Modes: Unlock The Secrets

By
Guitar Teacher
Dwayne Jenkins

Introduction

If you're the type of guitar player who wants to expand your musical vocabulary and enhance your improvisational skills, modes can help you get there. Guitar modes are created from the 7 notes of the major scale.

With each one starting on a different root note, they offer unique tone qualities and characteristics that can add a wealth of flavor to your playing. As they are used in a wide variety of musical styles.

What is great about the modes is that each one has a unique sequence of intervals that give them a very distinctive sound of their own. With practice, you get familiar with their patterns in different keys across the fretboard.

This not only helps you to master the modes individually but also enhances your fretboard knowledge, ear training, and music theory. Unlocking the secrets that will lead you to new dimensions of creativity and self-expression.

The interval note sequence can be broken down into a pattern (or scientific formula, if you will) of whole-steps and half-steps. And it's these patterns that give each one a distinctive musical voicing.

It is this distinctive voicing of each mode that will be explored in this training. You will learn and familiarize yourself with the note pattern of each mode and grasp its unique sound so that you can use it to create music of your own.

With this clear and concise, step-by-step method of study, you will discover a whole new world of possibilities. You'll just need the desire to <u>learn</u>, <u>study</u>, and <u>practice</u>. If you have that, there is no limit to what you can accomplish.

But you must have persistence and develop patience. As music is a language, and like all other languages, it will not come overnight. Only through daily application of what you learn will you unlock the secrets of the guitar modes.

So, grab your guitar and follow this guide like a map to a hidden treasure. Before you know it, you will be playing like you never thought possible. Good luck and don't forget to have fun.

Sincerely, Dwayne Jenkins

Table of Contents

Chapter 3 The Phrygian Mode 23

Chapter 4 The Lydian Mode 33

Chapter 5: The Mixolydian Mode 43

Chapter 6 The Aeolian Mode 53

Chapter 7 The Locrian Mode 63

Chapter 8: Chords Within The Modes 73

Guitar Modes Conclusion 87

Chapter 1 The Ionian Mode

Lesson 1: What is the Ionian mode

The Ionian mode is the first of the 7 modes discussed in this training. It is essentially the major scale and makes a place to start. Its structure is built on a series of whole and half steps. Its origins are rooted in Greek music.

In music, we start with the 12 notes of the musical alphabet. This is also considered to be the chromatic scale. Each note is right next to each other. These notes would be from A-G#.

A A# B C C# D D# E F F# G G#
1 2 3 4 5 6 7 8 9 10 11 12

And out of these 12 notes, we create the major scale. The sound of this scale will always be:

Do Re Mi Fa So La Ti Do
1   2 3 4 5 6 7 8

With the last note (in this example) being the same as the first. Just moving into the second octave to complete the musical cycle. So, technically, there are only 7 tone degrees that make up the scale.

As I said before, the Ionian mode is the major scale and should have the Do Re Mi sound to it. Let's look at this in more detail.

```
C major = C   D   E   F   G   A   B   C
           Do  Re  Mi  Fa  So  La  Ti  Do
```

If you go through these notes on your guitar, you will hear the Do Re Mi sound. This is the sound of the Ionian mode or the major scale. That is why these particular notes are chosen. All major scales (or Ionian modes) will have this tone structure.

As I stated before, what is great about the Ionian mode is that it is broken down into a series of whole steps and half steps.

What are whole steps and half steps?

They are note intervals. An interval is the distance between two notes. A half step is when two notes are right next to each other along the guitar fretboard, like A to A#. These two notes are 1 fret apart.

A whole step is a note interval of two frets, like A to B. These two notes are 2 frets apart from each other, with the A# note being between them.

Understand?

☐ **A half step is two notes one fret apart**
☐ **A whole note is two notes two frets apart**

This is important to know because it will help to understand the note formula for the Ionian mode. Which will help you to find the notes of any major scale.

Let's get back to the C major scale and see what the distance is between the notes. This will give us the note formula for the Ionian mode.

C major: C D E F G A B C
           W W H W W W H

As you can see from the above example, the major scale note formula is 2 whole steps a half step, 3 whole steps, and back to a half step.

  W W H W W W H
1 2 3 4 5 6 7 8

If you master this formula, not only will you be able to master the Ionian mode, but you will also be able to find the notes of any major scale.

4

Lesson 2: Characteristics of the Ionian mode

Now that you know the note formula, we can look at the characteristics of the Ionian mode. The personality of the notes structure.

When you line up the notes in this step sequence, you get a happy and bright tone. A very optimistic character. Like someone who is happy and feels good.

Knowing this helps in creating a composition that has this character to it. It also helps with recognizing a song that has a happy sound to it. If it does, it is more than likely written in a major key.

The reason why this is such is that the Ionian mode consists of a natural 3rd, perfect 5th, and major 7th note. These note intervals give it its character.

Natural 3rd = bright and uplifting
Perfect 5th = provides stability
Major 7th = Adds a sense of tension

When you change these characteristics of the mode (as we will be doing with the other 6), you will see how it affects the overall sound of each mode. Remember, Ionian is happy.

Lesson 3: The Ionian mode in different keys

Now that you've learned about the note structure of the Ionian mode and the character it creates, you can learn where it is located in different keys.

The best way to do this is to recognize the scale pattern of this mode. Once we do this, we can then just move it up and down the fretboard to change key locations. This is where the rubber meets the road.

G Ionian mode:

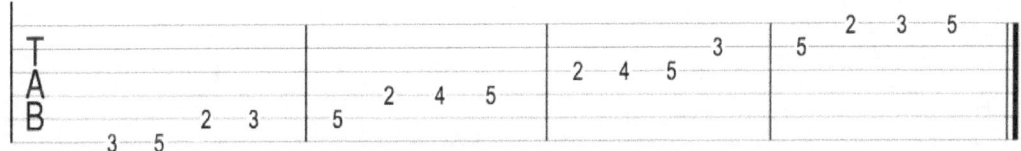

This is the Ionian mode written in tab. If you're not familiar with tabs, the lines represent the 6 guitar strings with your low E on the bottom. The numbers indicate the frets.

If you start on the 3rd fret and go through the mode, you will hear the Do Re Mi. Get familiar with this pattern as well as its sound.

Now let's look at it in other keys.

6

Here it is in a few more keys along the fretboard.

A Ionian mode:

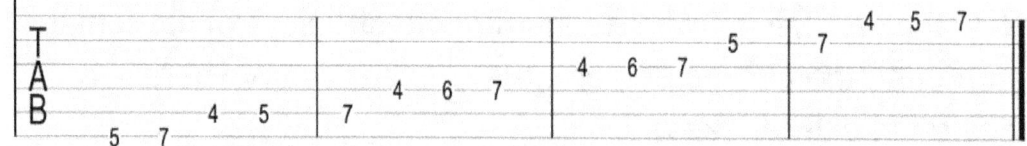

B Ionian mode:

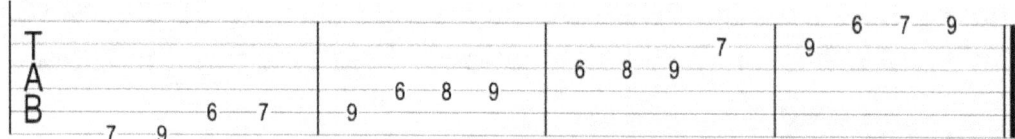

C Ionian Mode

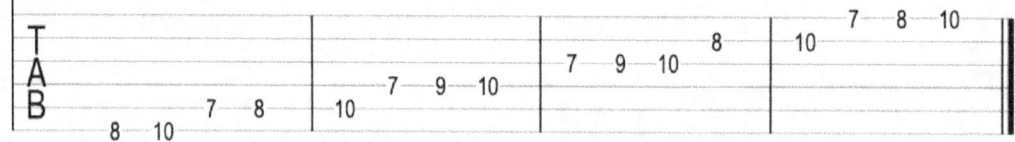

D Ionian mode

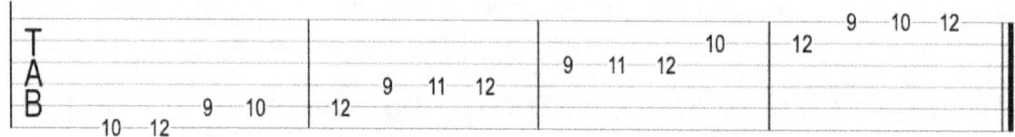

Go through this mode and notice that the pattern is always the same. It is just where it is located along the fretboard that changes keys. Find other keys to play this in.

Lesson 4: Ionian mode guitar licks

Now that you know the Ionian mode pattern across the fretboard and can play it in multiple keys, you want to learn how to use it in music. Do this with Ionian mode guitar licks.

To get the most out of this lesson, be sure to study reading guitar notation. It would be best if you already understand such techniques as hammer-ons, pull-offs, slides, etc. It is these techniques that will bring the modes to life.

These examples will be in the key of G at the 3rd fret. I recommend you try them out in other keys to get familiar with how they sound in those locations.

Guitar lick #1:

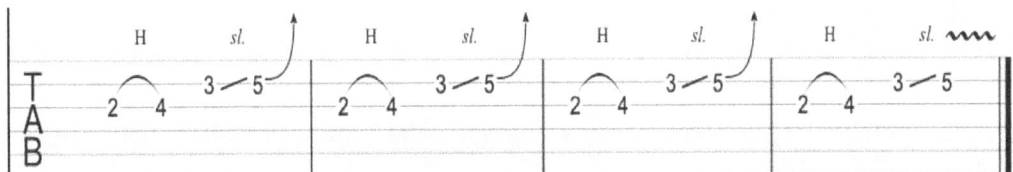

In this example, you use a hammer on the 2nd fret third string, a slide on the 3rd fret second string, a bend on the 5th fret second string, and a vibrato at the end of the lick.

As you practice this lick, visualize where it is located in the Ionian mode.

8

Guitar lick #2:

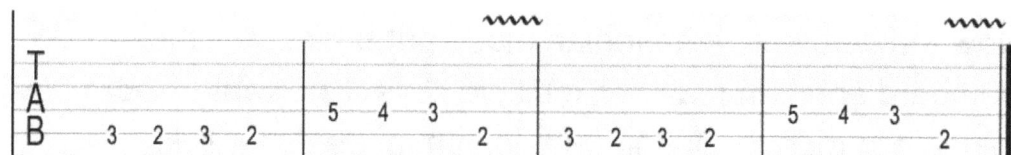

This lick is a little different. It goes through the mode in a sequence of notes and has a vibrato at the end.

Guitar Lick #3:

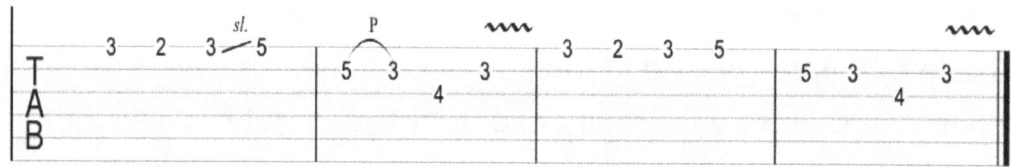

This lick involves a slide, a pull-off, and a vibrato at the end. Notice how the vibrato makes a nice expression at the end.

Guitar Lick #4:

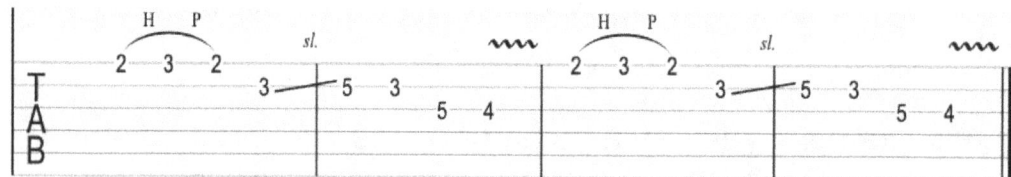

This lick uses a hammer-on pull-off, a slide, and a vibrato at the end. Also, work at making up your own from these examples, and don't forget to try them out in other keys.

Lesson 5: Chapter 1 Quiz

In this first chapter, you learned about the Ionian mode. What it is, its character, playing it in different keys, and some guitar licks you can play within it.

This is a great way to make sure that you know the material and are ready for the next chapter. Have fun and good luck.

Q: What is the Ionian mode?

A: _____

Q: How many notes are in the music alphabet?

A: _____

Q: What is another name for the music alphabet?

A: _____

Q: What is the sound of the major scale?

A: _____

Q: What is a whole step?

A: _____

Q: What is a half-step?

A: _____

Q: What is the note formula for the Ionian mode?

A: _____

Q: How many whole steps are in the Ionian mode?

A: _____

Q: What kind of character does the Ionian mode have?

A: _____

Q: What kind of 3rd note does the Ionian mode have?

A: _____

Q: What kind of 5th note does the Ionian mode have?

A: _____

Q: What kind of 7th note does the Ionian mode have?

A; _____

Q: What do guitar licks accomplish?

A; _____

By knowing the answers to these questions, you increase your knowledge of the fretboard and the concepts in this chapter. Do this, and you will be ahead of most guitarists.

Chapter 1 Summary

In this first chapter, you learned about the 1st of the 7 modes. The Ionian mode. This is a great place to start because it will be the first brick in your mode's foundation.

We first looked at what the Ionian mode is. Essentially, the major scale has a structure that is built on a series of whole steps and half steps. Comes from Greek origins.

Then, we learn about the characteristics of the Ionian mode. Since the notes line up the way they do, it has the Do Re Mi sound. This gives it a bright and happy tone. Which is good for key recognition and song composition.

Third, we look at how this mode lays out across the fretboard and where to play it in different keys. This is helpful to know so it can be played in any key. Not only does this help with your compositions, but it also helps with fretboard mastery.

Lastly, you learn guitar licks. This is what brings the mode to life. Study this chapter, as it will set the foundation for what's to come with the other modes.

12

Chapter 2 The Dorian Mode

Lesson 6: What is the Dorian mode?

The Dorian mode is the second of the 7 modes. The mode is based on the 2nd tone degree of the major scale that it comes out of.

In the key of G major, the Dorian mode will be in A.

Key of G major: G A B C D E F# G
Ionian mode = 1 2 3 4 5 6 7 8

A Dorian in G major: A B C D E F# G A
Dorian mode =   1 2 b3 4 5 6 b7 8

We learned in the last chapter that the Ionian mode has a natural 3rd and a major 7th. As you can see from above, the Dorian mode has a flat 3rd and a flat 7, and it is these notes that make this mode different from the Ionian.

Whenever you have a scale or chord that has a flat 3rd note, it becomes a minor. Something to take note of when composing music.

Since the Dorian mode has a flat 3rd and flat 7, this tells us that it is a minor mode.

From the example above, we can see where the Dorian mode is in the major scale. So, if you were in the key of C major, where is the Dorian mode going to be located?

Let's take a look.

C major: C D E F G A B C

Since the Ionian mode is the 1st tone degree, it will start on the C note. Since the Dorian mode is the 2nd tone degree, it will start on the 2nd note of the scale. In the scale of C major, the 2nd note is a D. This would make it the D Dorian mode.

Make sense?

This concept works with all the major scales. This is what is great about the modes. Since there are 7 different tone degrees of the major scale, and a mode is based on each note, we can create 7 different modes.

This gives a wide variety of things we can do with them. We can use them for melodies, chords, and progressions in our songs or use them to get a better understanding of the guitar fretboard.

Remember, what is also great about the modes is that each one of them has a different character.

Lesson 7: Characteristics of the Dorian mode

Since we now know that the Dorian mode is based on the 2nd note in the key it comes out of, we can find it in any key we choose to play in. Having a flat 3rd and a flat 7th is what makes it unique to the Ionian mode.

As a minor mode, it is going to have the characteristics of a sad, somber type of sound.

Ionian mode = 1 2 3 4 5 6 7 8
                  W W H W W W H

Dorian mode = 1 2 b3 4 5 6 b7 8
                  W H W W W H W

If you look at the two whole-step and half-step formulas, the half steps change location. This is because of the flt 3rd and flat 7th notes of the Dorian mode.

Flat 3rd = softer, minor quality.
Perfect 5th = a strong foundation.
Flat 7th = adds a bluesy element.

Remember, it is all about changing the note formula that gives each mode its character. This is what you want to master with each mode.

Lesson 8: The Dorian mode in different keys

Now that we know a few things about the Dorian mode, the note formula, and its characteristics, we can look into playing it in different keys.

Since we used the key of G major for the Ionian, we'll stay in that key. Since the Ionian mode is formed off of the G note, then the Dorian will be formed off of the A note.

A Dorian mode:

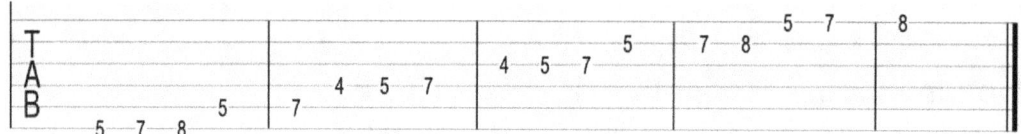

In the key of G major, this mode will start at the 5th fret. The reason for this is that is where the A note is located along the fretboard, and since the Dorian mode is the second mode, it will start here in this key.

Study this pattern, it is the same in any key you choose to play it along the fretboard. You just need to master the pattern of the mode and where to play it in any key. Just like you learned with the Ionian mode.

Let's take a look at its location in a few more keys.

B Dorian mode:

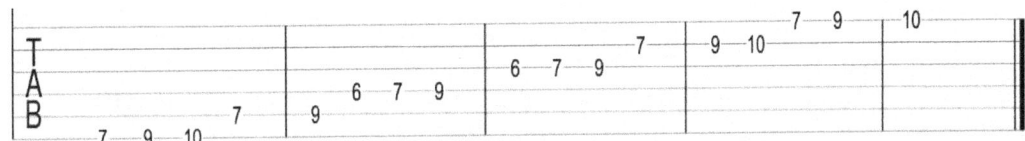

C Dorian mode:

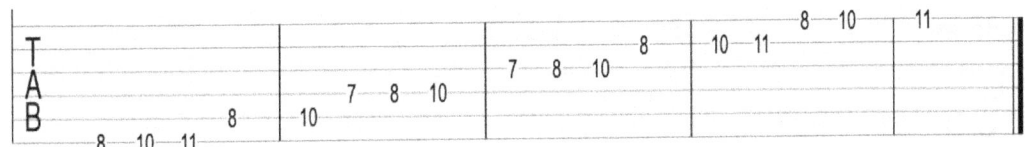

D Dorian mode:

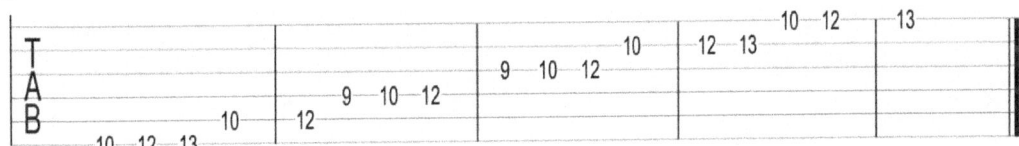

E Dorian mode:

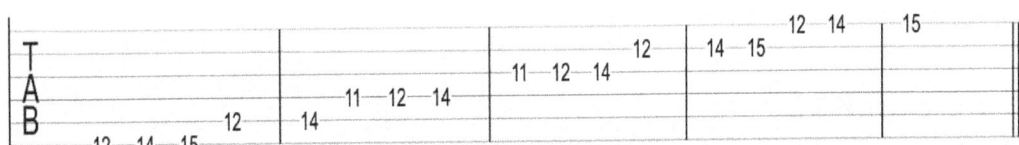

Notice how these are all the same pattern. This is what's great about learning guitar: the fretboard can be broken down into patterns. Remember this, as it will be helpful along your journey to guitar greatness.

18

Lesson 9: Dorian mode guitar licks

Just like with the Ionian mode, we now want to learn some guitar licks that we can play in the Dorian mode. This will help us to get the most out of it.

These will be presented in A Dorian.

Guitar Lick #1:

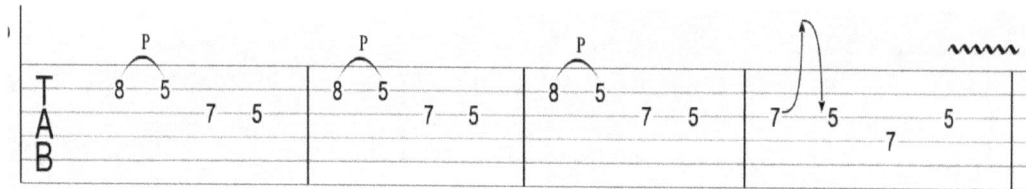

This lick has a pull-off on the 8th fret second string and a string bend release on the 7th fret third string, with vibrato at the end on the 5th fret third string.

Guitar Lick #2:

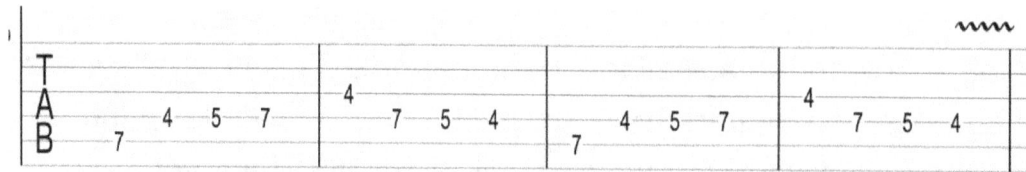

This lick is a simple repeated melody line that has a vibrato on the 4th fret fourth string.

Guitar lick #3:

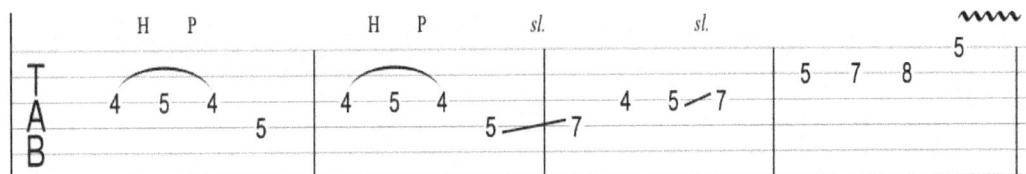

This lick consists of a hammer-on pull-off at the 4th fret third string, a slide at the 5th fret fourth string, 5th fret third string, and a vibrato on the 5th fret first string.

Guitar Lick #4:

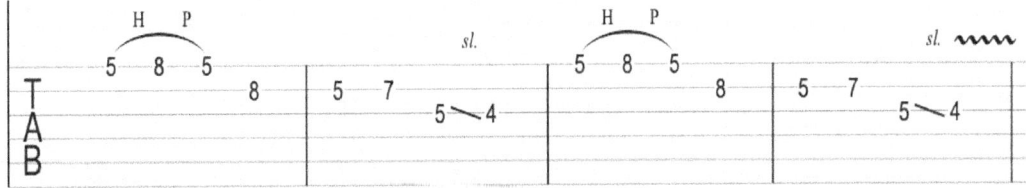

Guitar lick #5:

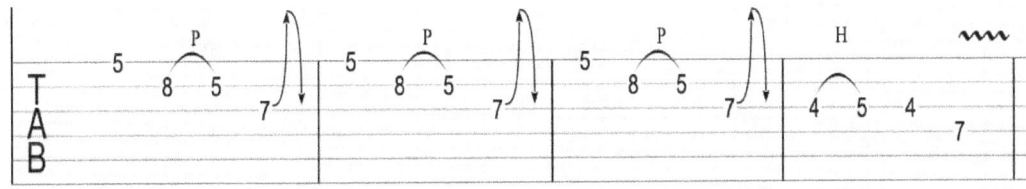

Practice these licks daily, and once you get them down, play them in other keys along the fretboard.

Lesson 10: Chapter 2 Quiz

Here I present you with a quiz for chapter two. The Dorian mode.

Remember, these learning assessments are for your benefit, so take them lightly and have fun with them.

Q: What is the Dorian mode?
A: _____

Q: What number position is it within the key it comes out of?
A: _____

Q: What is the whole-step half-step formula?
A: _____

Q: What notes are flat in the Dorian mode?
A: _____

Q: What kind of sound does the Dorian mode produce?
A: _____

Q: In the key of C major, the Dorian mode is where?
A: _____

Q: In the key of G major, the Dorian mode is where?

A: _____

Q: What kind of 5th does the Dorian mode have?

A: _____

Q: The B Dorian mode is in what key?

A: _____

Q: The D Dorian mode is in what key?

A: _____

Q: What techniques are used in guitar lick #1?

A: _____

Q: What techniques are used in guitar lick #4?

A: _____

Q: What techniques are used in guitar lick #5?

A: _____

This chapter will set up a sound foundation. Remember, if you don't know an answer, go back and find it in the lessons and write it down here. This will help you to retain the information and get a better understanding of the Dorian mode.

Chapter 2 Summary

In chapter two, we have learned about the second of the 7 modes. The Dorian mode.

We first look at what the Dorian mode is. This mode, like the Ionian, is made up of a series of whole steps and half steps. This one is different from the Ionian because it has a flat 3rd and flat 7th note.

Since it has a flat 3rd note, it is considered a minor mode. This is something to remember in music: Anytime you have a flat 3rd note in a scale or chord, it is minor, and a minor has a sad, moody sound.

We also learn about the note pattern across the fretboard in multiple keys. This is important to know as it will allow you to know how to play the mode and where it is located.

Lastly, we look at ways to play the mode through guitar licks. This is where the rubber meets the road. This is how you bring the mode to life. Make sure to take time daily to master these in different keys.

This is how you make the mode sound like music.

Chapter 3 The Phrygian Mode

Lesson 11: What is the Phrygian mode

The Phrygian mode is the 3rd of the 7 modes of the major scale. It provides a unique tonal quality that is different from the other two modes that we have looked at. The reason for this is the whole-step and half-step formula.

In the key of G major, the Phrygian mode will be in B.

Key of G major: G A B C D E F# G
Ionian mode = 1 2 3 4 5 6 7 8

B Phrygian in G major: B C D E F# G A B
Phrygian mode =   1 b2 b3 4 5 b6 b7 8

Since the B Phrygin comes out of the key of G major, it uses the same notes, just like the Dorian mode. But this time, it starts on the 3rd note, the B. When we go through the B Phrygian mode, we can tell it is also a minor mode.

This is because it has a flat 3rd note in it. It also has a flat 7th like the Dorian mode. What makes this minor mode different than Dorian is the other two flat notes.

The Phrygin mode also consists of the flat 2 and the flat 6.

What is the whole-step, half-step formula for this mode?

Well, let's take a look.

```
B Phrygian:  B  C  D  E  F#  G  A  B
             1  2  3  4  5   6  7  8
             H  W  W  W  H   W  W
```

From the example above, we can see that this mode starts with a half step. Not only that, but the half steps in this mode are between the 1st and 2nd and the 5th and 6th notes. It is this change in note structure that gives it a different sound.

Remember, it is through note manipulation that we can create distinctive sounds out of the Ionian mode through the creation of 6 others. The Phrygian being the 3rd.

Look at where the half steps are in the other two modes that we learned in previous lessons.

Ionian mode =   **W W H W W W H**
Dorian mode =   **W H W W W H W**
Phrygian mode = **H W W W H W W**

Can you see how this change in the note intervals makes up these different modes, even though they all use the same notes?

Lesson 12: Characteristics of the Phrygian mode

What is great about the Phrygian mode is that the note intervals produce an exotic, dark sound that is different than the other minor mode we learned, the Dorian mode.

A Dorian: **1 2 b3 4 5 6 b7**

B Phrygian: **1 b2 b3   4 5 b6 b7**

Both of these modes have the flat 3rd note, so this tells us that they are both minor, but the Phrygian also has the flat 2nd and the flat 6th, and it is these two notes that make it a different type of minor mode.

A mode that has characteristics different from those of the Dorian. You want to fully understand these details when choosing which one to use in composition. The shade of color you want to use when painting your musical landscape.

Work on switching between these two minor modes when practicing them. As you do, you will begin to hear the difference between them. As if they are two shades of the same color. The minor color.

Let's take a look at all three modes learned so far and see the difference between them. This will make sure that we get a full understanding.

Ionian mode: 1 2 3 4 5 6 7   8 = major (natural 3rd)
              G A B C D E F# G

Dorian mode: 1 2 b3 4 5   6 b7 8 = minor (flat 3rd)
              A B C   D E F# G A

Phrygian mode: 1 b2 b3 4 5 b6 b7 8 = minor (flat 3rd)
                 B C   D   E F# G A B

In the above example, we can see the note difference of these three modes and why they are as such. The Ionian is a major, and the other two are minor. This is very helpful when creating chords and solos.

Flat 2nd = Distinct tone from other minor modes.
Flat 3rd = Provides a somber, moody quality.
Perfect 5th = Stability against the mode's exotic tension.

Remember, it is these qualities of the mode that give the Phrygian its character and should be exploited when using it in composition.

Lesson 13: The Phrygian mode in different keys

Now that we have learned a few things about the Phrygian mode, we can look into understanding how it lays across the fretboard in different keys.

Since we have been using the key of G major for the modes, we'll stay in that key. We learned that the Ionian mode is formed off of the G note, and the Phrygian will be formed off of the B note.

B Phrygian mode:

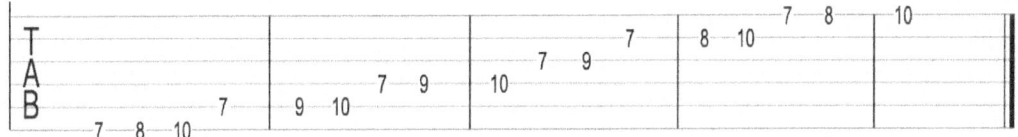

This mode will start on the 7th fret because that is where the B note is. In fact, once you learn your notes along the fretboard, you can begin to this mode anywhere there is a B note.

Remember, since the Phrygian mode is the 3rd mode, it will always start on the 3rd note of the key it comes out of. In this example of G major, it is at the B note.

When learning these in different keys, try to determine what key the mode is being played in.

C Phrygian mode:

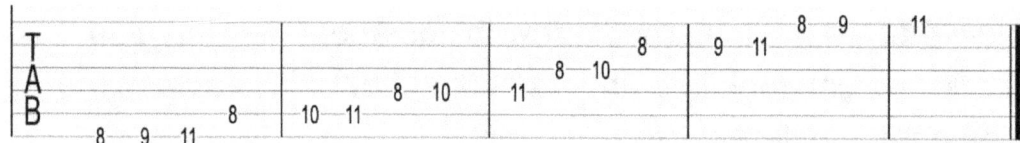

D Phrygian mode:

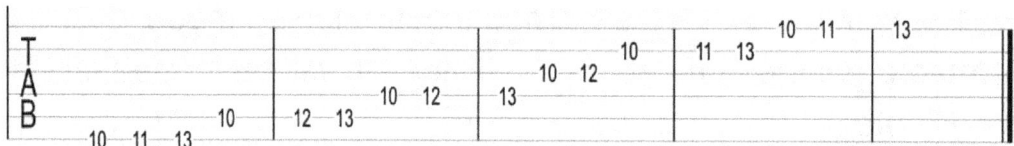

E Phrygian mode:

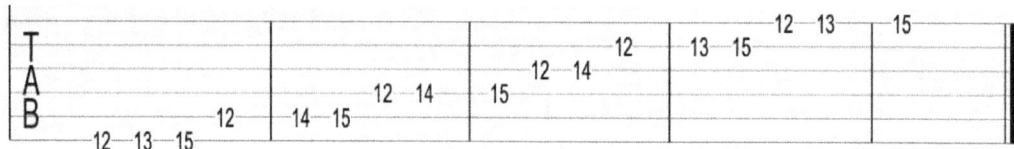

F# Phrygian mode:

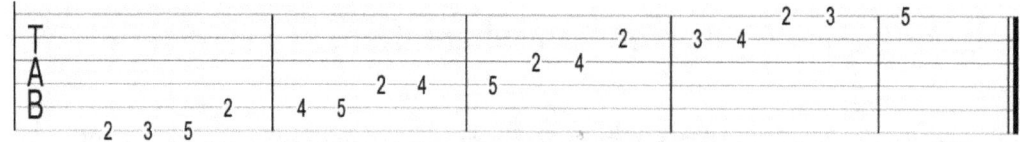

Notice how all these patterns are the same. Just in different locations along the fretboard.

I put the F# Phrygin at the 2nd fret just for easier playing, but remember, it can also be played at the 14th fret as well.

Lesson 14: Phrygian mode guitar licks

As with the other modes learned so far, we want to be able to turn this pattern of notes into music. This is where guitar licks come in.

Remember, guitar licks are phrases of notes that bring the modes to life and make them sound musical.

Guitar Lick #1:

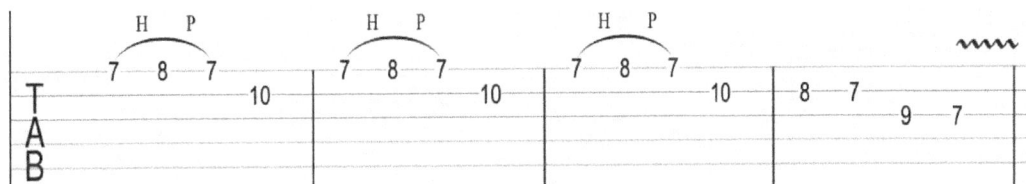

In this example, we start with a hammer-on pul-off on the 7th fret and move to the 10th fret, repeat it three times, add a few extra notes, and end the lick on the 7th fret with vibrato.

Guitar Lick #2:

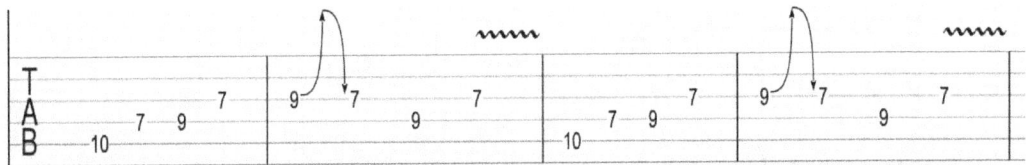

This lick utilizes a bend release at the 9th fret and ends with a vibrato at the 7th, played twice.

30

Guitar Lick #3:

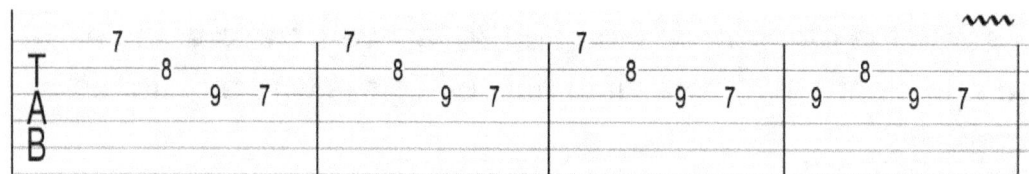

In this example, we move through the mode diagonally from the 7th fret, repeat it three times, add a few more notes, and end with a vibrato on the 7th fret.

Guitar Lick #4:

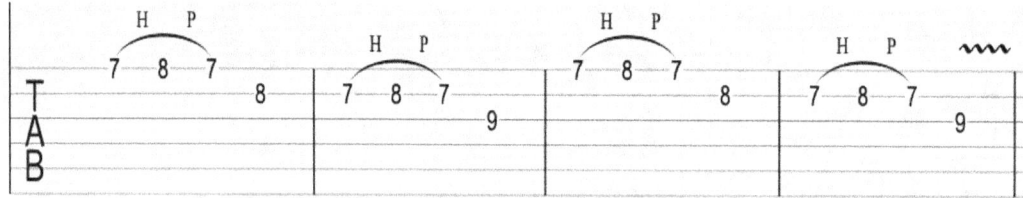

Guitar Lick #5:

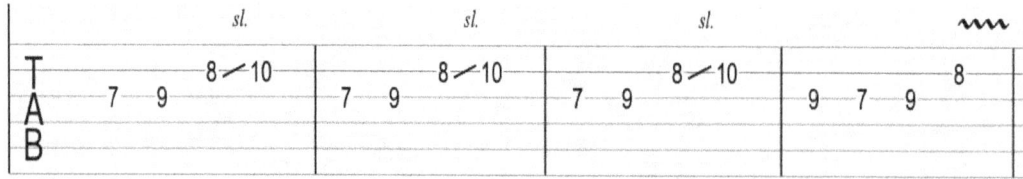

All these examples use techniques associated with lead guitar playing.   Learn them, expand on them, and then create unique licks of your own.

Lesson 15:   Chapter 3 Quiz

In this chapter, we have learned a lot about the Phrygian mode. Here is a little learning assessment to see how you did and what still needs to be worked on.

Q: The Phrygian mode is what number of the 7 modes?

A: _____

Q: What is the whole-step half-step formula?

A: _____

Q: In the key of G major, where is the Phrygian mode located?

A: _____

Q: Is the Phrygin a major or minor mode?

A: _____

Q: What key is D Phrygian in?

A: _____

Q: Why are guitar licks important to learn?

A: _____

Make sure to study the Phrygian mode. It will be a huge benefit to you as you progress in your studies.

Chapter 3 summary

In chapter three, we have learned about the 3rd of the 7 modes. The Phrygian mode. This is a different type of mode from the previous two because of the whole-step and half-step formula. Like the other two, this gives it its unique tone quality.

First, we learn that in the key of G major (which is the key we are working out of in this training), the Phrygian mode is located at the B note. This is called B Phrygian and uses the same notes as G major.

Second, we learn that the Phrygian mode is minor. How do we know this? Because it has a flat 3rd note in it. In addition to that, it also has flat 2nd, 6th, and 7th notes. And it is these additional flat notes that make up its character.

Third, we look at the way this mode lays across the fretboard in a pattern. We also learn that this pattern stays the same when we play it in different locations, and it is these different locations that determine what key we play it in.

Lastly, we look at guitar licks that can be played out of the Phrygian mode. Although these are presented in B Phrygian, I recommend you play them in different keys along the fretboard.

Chapter 4 The Lydian Mode

Lesson 16: What is the Lydian mode

The Lydian mode is the 4th of the 7th modes, and because of the way the notes line up, it is considered a major mode. But it is different than the Ionian mode.

Why?

Well, let's take a look.

Sticking with the key of G major, we look to the fourth note to locate and create the Lydian mode. This note in the key of G major is the C note. So in G major, we would have the C Lydian mode.

Key of G major: G A B C D E F# G
Ionian mode = 1 2 3 4 5 6 7 8

C Lydian in G major: C D E F# G A B C
Lydian mode =   1 2 3 #4 5 6 7 8

Once again, we can see that the same notes are being used, and in the same order, but instead of starting on the G note, we start with the C note. This creates a variation of the major scale.

Since it has the natural 3rd note in it, we can conclude that it is a major mode. We can also conclude that, although it is major, it has a different sound quality to it.

We now have two major modes to work with, the Ionian mode and the Lydian mode, and two minor modes to work with, the Dorian and the Phrygian.

What is great about the Lydian mode is that it has a nice uplifting sound like the Ionian, except its tone quality is a bit different. This mode evokes a sense of wonder and exploration.

If you were writing a song that conveyed a happy emotion, but you wanted to add a sense of excitement, you would want to use the Lydian mode instead of the Ionian,

Knowing what mood each mode can produce is what making music is all about. Being in control of the listener's emotion. This is what all the great composers of all styles of music learn to master.

By diving into what the Lydian mode is and how to use it in song, you will be doing the same thing. You will be able to direct the emotions of the listener. Just as your emotion is being directed by composers when you listen to their music.

Lesson 17: Characteristics of the Lydian mode

In the last lesson, we discovered a few things about the Lydian mode. It is a major mode like the Ionian, and it produces a sense of wonder and exploration.

This comes from the whole-step and half-step formula of the notes within the mode. It is this scientific formula that gives it its character and personality.

Let's take a look at this in further detail.

```
              G  A  B   C  D  E  F#  G
Ionian mode:  1  2  3   4  5  6  7   8
              W  W  H   W  W  W  H
```

```
              C  D  E  F#  G  A  B  C
Lydian mode:  1  2  3  #4  5  6  7  8
              W  W  W   H  W  W  H
```

Can you see how this works? Since we start on the C note, it raises the 4th in the C Lydian mode. The F# at the 4th position in the Lydian mode makes it raised, but in the 7th position of the Ionian mode, it stays natural.

This is the difference between these two major modes.

The sharp 4th gives the Lydian mode a very distinct sound that is different from the Ionian mode, and like the Dorian and Phrygian modes, you want to exploit this when using it.

Let's take a look at all four modes so far.

Ionian mode: 1 2 3 4 5 6 7   8 = major (natural 3rd)
               G A B C D E F# G

Dorian mode: 1 2 b3 4 5 6 b7 8 = minor (flat 3rd)
               A B C   D E F# G A

Phrygian mode: 1 b2 b3 4 5 b6 b7 8 = minor (flat 3rd)
                 B C D   E F# G A B

Lydian mode: 1 2 3 #4 5 6 7 8 = major (natural 3rd)
               C D E F# G A B C

Study these modes. Write them down on a piece of paper and determine the whole-step and half-step formula for each. The more you do this, the more it will sink in and become beneficial to your musical advancement.

Now, let's look at how the Lydian mode lays across the fretboard and in different keys.

Lesson 18: The Lydian mode in different keys

Now that we know a few things about what the Lydian mode is and its character, let's look at how it lays across the fretboard.

Once again, since we are in the key of G major (for easier learning), we will present it at the C position.

C Lydian mode:

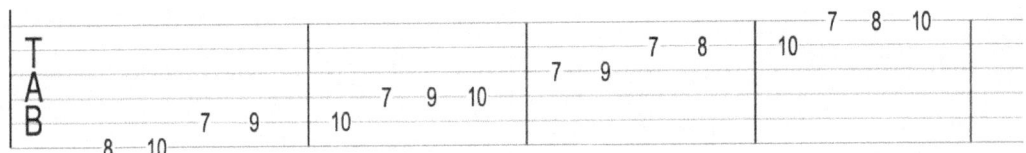

This mode will start on the 8th fret because that is where the C note is. If you look at it closely, you will see that it is the same pattern of notes as the Phrygian, except it starts on the C note because it is the 4th mode.

Also, because we move up one fret to the C note, it now becomes a major mode. Why? Because of the way the whole-step and half-steps line up. Because of this slight variation, we get a completely different sound.

Let's take a look at this mode in a few more keys.

D Lydian mode:

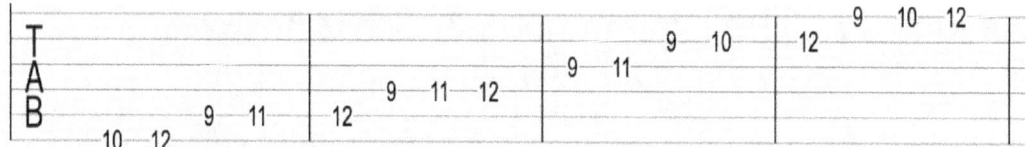

E Lydian mode:

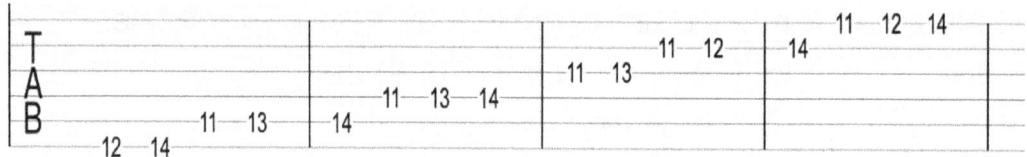

F# Lydian mode:

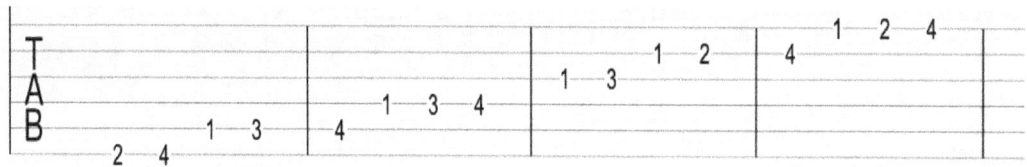

G Lydian mode:

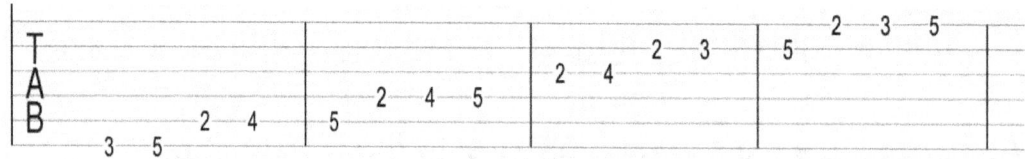

Just like before, with all the other modes, the pattern of notes stays the same. It's just where you play it along the fretboard that determines the key it's played in.

Lesson 19: Lydian mode guitar licks

Now, we come to the fun part. Guitar licks within the Lydian mode. C Lydian in the key of G major.

Guitar Lick #1:

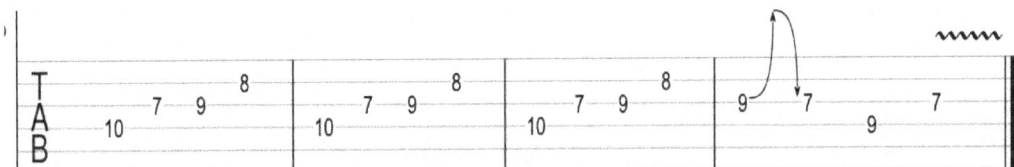

In this example, we use a repeated lick with a bend release and vibrato at the end.

Guitar Lick #2:

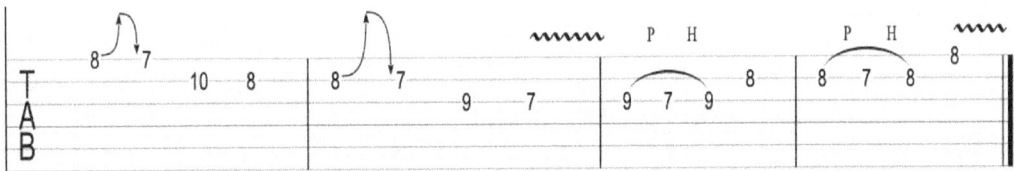

In this example, we use a bend release with vibrato and a hammer-on pull-off.

These are all common techniques used for lead guitar playing, so make sure you master them. As you will hear, they make the scale sound musical.

40

Guitar Lick #3:

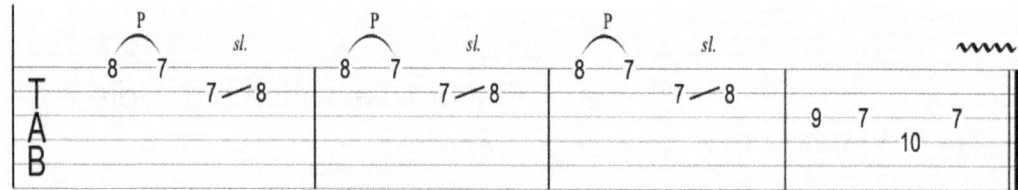

In this example, we use a pull-off, slides, and vibrato at the end.

Guitar Lick #4:

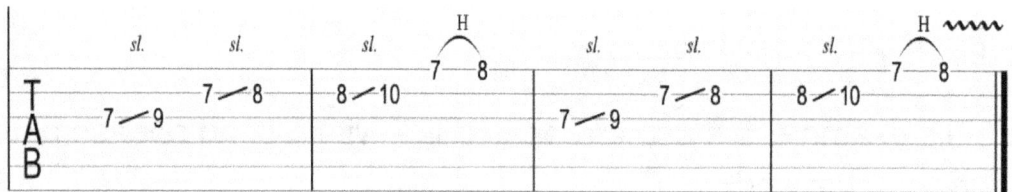

In this example, we use slides, a hammer-on, and vibrato.

Guitar Lick #5:

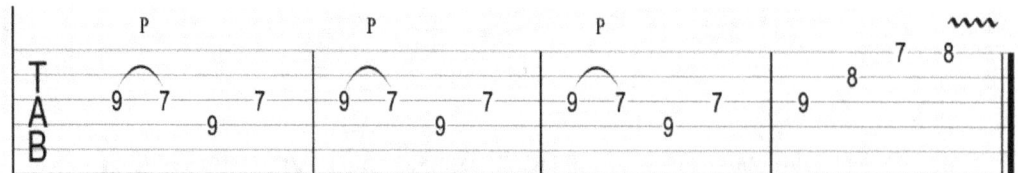

Another example of pull-offs, repeated licks, and vibrato.

Once you learn these, expand on them and play them in different locations to master the fretboard.

Lesson 20: Chapter 4 Quiz

In this chapter, we have learned a lot about the Lydian mode, and once again, a learning assessment to see what you've learned and what still needs to be worked on is presented.

Q: What is the Lydian mode?

A: _____

Q: Is the Lydian mode major or minor?

A: _____

Q: What is the note formula for the Lydian mode?

A: _____

Q: How is the Lydian mode different from the Ionian?

A: _____

Q: What is the sound of the Lydian mode?

A: _____

Q: What note is the Lydian mode located in G major?

A: _____

Q: What key is the E Lydian mode in?

A: _____

Chapter 4 Summary

In chapter four, we have learned about the 4th of the 7 modes. The Lydian mode. This is another major mode, but unique in the fact that it has a sharp fourth, which gives it a different sound than the Ionian mode.

First, we learn that in the key of G major, the Lydian mode is the 4th mode located at the C note. This is the C Lydian mode and, like the other modes, Ionian, Dorian, and Phrygian, it uses the same notes but a different note sequence.

Second, we learn that the Lydian mode is a major mode because it has a natural 3rd note in it. But, it is different than the Ionian mode because it has a sharp 4th note in it, and it is this sharp note that gives it a unique character.

Third, we look at the way the Lydian mode lays across the fretboard. We also learn how this pattern remains the same when played in different locations. We also learn that the name changes from C Lydian to D Lydian, to E Lydian, etc.

Lastly, we look at guitar licks that can be played within the Lydian mode. I recommend you play them in different keys, as they will help you to increase your knowledge of the mode.

Chapter 5 The Mixolydian Mode

Lesson 21: What is the Mixolydian mode?

Now we come to the 5th mode of the 7, the Mixolydian mode. This mode is also a major mode. What makes it major? That's right, a natural 3rd note.

What makes this major mode unique from the other two, the Ionian and the Lydian, is the fact that it has a flat 7 note in it, and it is this flat 7th note that gives it its sound.

In the key of G major, the Mixolydian mode will be in D.

Key of G major: G A B C D E F# G
Ionian mode = 1 2 3 4 5 6 7 8

D Mixolydian in G major: D E F# G A B C D
Mixolydian mode =   1 2 3 4 5 6 b7 8

As you can see from the way the notes line up in the above example, the Mixolydian mode has a natural 3rd and flat 7th. It is almost exactly like the Ionian and the Lydian.

Can you see how the movement of just one note can make a difference? The Phrygian is minor, but if you move over just one note, you have the Lydian major.

Ionian mode = 1 2 3 4 5 6 7 8

Lydian = 1 2 3 #4 5 6 7 8

Mixolydian = 1 2 3 4 5 6 b7 8

See how these three major modes are the same but different. It is this difference that gives them their character. It is this character that allows you to determine which one to use at any given time when creating music.

What is great about the Mixolydian mode is the flat 7th note gives its dominant quality. This is helpful to know because it tells us that it can be used over dominant chords.

Why?

Because dominant chords have a flat 7th in them as well. Like a C7, G7, D7, etc. If you were to create a chord progression using these three chords and play the Mixolydian mode over the top in the proper key, you would see that it fits.

*Remember, a song doesn't have to be complicated, and it doesn't need to have a lot of chords in it to be effective. Many great songs only have three chords in them.

Think about this when it comes to composing your music.

Lesson 22: Characteristics of the Mixolydian mode

With the Mixolydian mode having a flat 7th note, it often conveys a more relaxed and bluesy tone quality. Unlike the Lydian mode, which conveys more of a tone of wonder and exploration.

Knowing the difference between these two modes and the emotions that they produce allows you to choose which one will be best for the music you are writing.

Let's look at the Mixolydian mode in more detail.

```
                G A B  C D E F# G
Ionian mode:  1 2 3  4 5 6 7  8
                W W H W W W  H


                 D E F# G A  B  C D
Mixolydian mode:  1 2 3  4 5  6  b7 8
                  W W H  W W  H  W
```

As you can see from the above example, the Mixolydian mode is the same as the Ionian, except for the flat 7th note. It is this flat 7th note that allows it to produce the sound that it does.

As I said with the previous modes, you want to find out what makes the mode unique (in this case, the flat 7th) and exploit it to bring out its character.

Let's take a look at all five modes so far.

Ionian mode: 1 2 3 4 5 6 7   8 = major (natural 3rd)
            G A B C D E F# G

Dorian mode: 1 2 b3 4 5   6 b7 8 = minor (flat 3rd)
           A B C   D E F# G A

Phrygian mode: 1 b2 b3 4 5 b6 b7 8 = minor (flat 3rd)
              B C   D E F# G A B

Lydian mode: 1 2 3 #4 5 6 7 8 = major (natural 3rd)
           C D E F# G A B C

Mixolydian mode: 1 2 3 4 5 6 b7 8 = major (natural 3rd)
             D E F# G A B C D

Can you see how when the notes line up in the D Mixolydian mode, the C becomes the flat 7th note?

This is how you get the most out of the notes within a key. This example is in the key of G major, but it works with all 12 keys in the music alphabet.

Lesson 23: The Mixolydian mode in different keys

Now, let's take a look at the Mixolydian mode as it lays across the fretboard. As with the other modes, we will learn where it will be located in other keys as well.

Since we are in the key of G major, the Mixolydian mode will be D Mixolydian.

D Mixolydian mode:

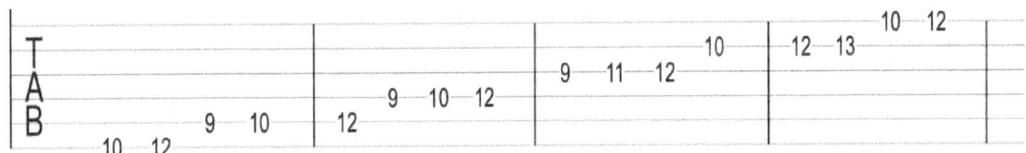

This mode will start on the 10th fret because that is where the D note is. This mode is unique not only by the note structure but also by the fact that it steps out of the box pattern. Learning to see these small details can help you learn faster.

This is also a major mode. Why? Because of the way the whole-step and half-steps line up. As we learned in previous lessons, this mode has a natural 3rd and a flat 7th.

Let's look at this in other keys along the fretboard.

E Mixolydian mode:

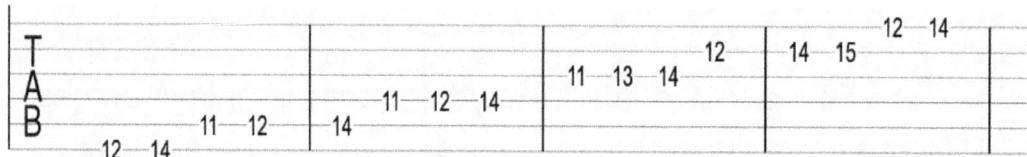

F# Mixolydian mode:

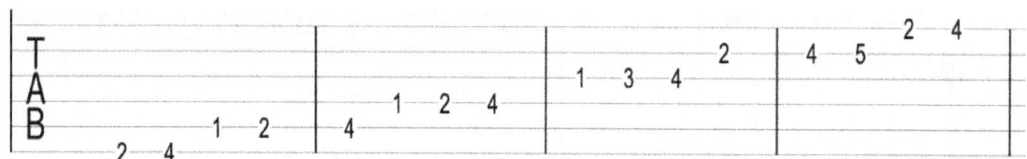

G Mixolydian mode:

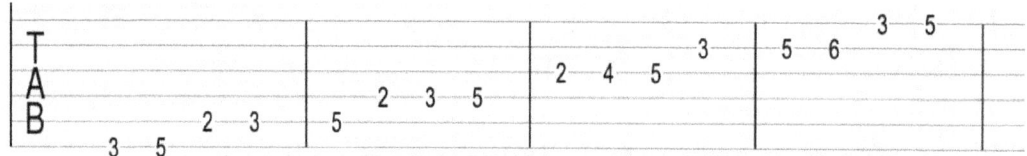

A Mixolydian mode:

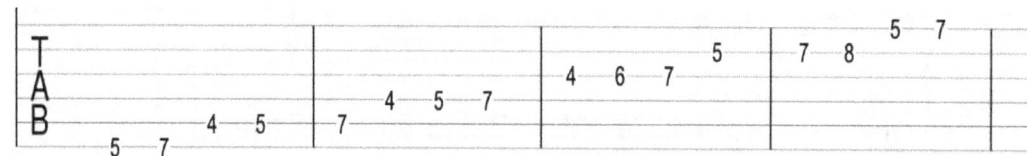

Once again, these are the same patterns in different locations. Remember that the fretboard can be divided into patterns, and if you think this way, it will be easier to learn.

Lesson 24: Mixolydian mode guitar licks

Just like with the other modes, we now want to learn some guitar licks that we can play to make it sound musical. This is a very important aspect of the modes.

These will be presented in D Mixolydian.

.

Guitar Lick #1:

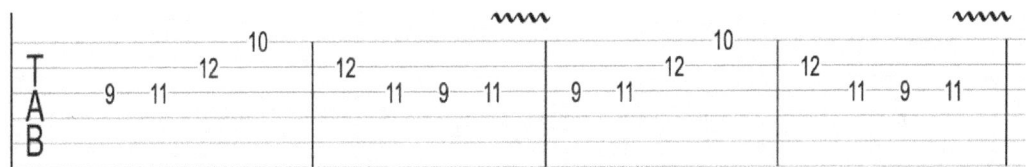

In this example, we use a repeated lick and end it with vibrato. This is a great way to create an intro melody line that can catch the listeners' attention.

Guitar Lick #2:

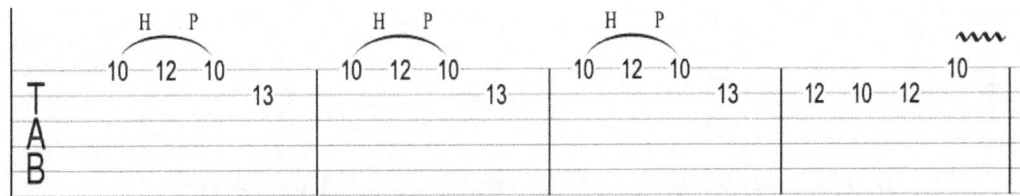

This example uses a hammer-on pull-off, with a repeated lick and a vibrato at the end. Remember, if a lick sounds good to you, repeat it. Listen for this technique in your favorite songs.

50

Guitar Lick #3:

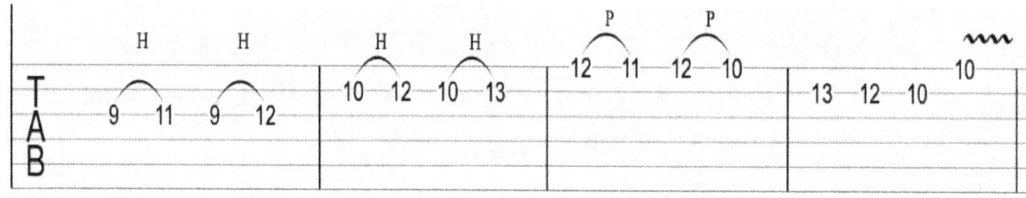

In this example, we use hammer-ons and pull-offs and end the lick with vibrato.

Guitar Lick #4:

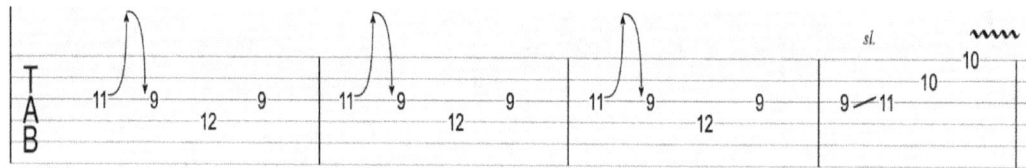

This example uses a bend release, a slide, and a vibrato.

Guitar Lick #5:

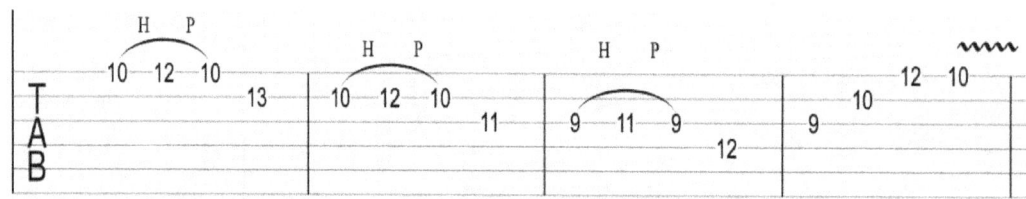

This example uses hammer-on pull-offs and vibrato.

Remember, these are techniques that you want to master no matter where you choose to play them along the fretboard.

Lesson 25: Chapter 5 Quiz

In this chapter, we have learned about the Mixolydian mode. What it is, and what makes it unique. Let's assess how well we learned the lessons and retained the information within them.

Q: What is the Mixolydian mode?

A: _____

Q: Is the Mixolydian mode major or minor?

A: _____

Q: What is the note formula for the Mixolydian mode?

A: _____

Q: What is the sound of the Mixolydian mode?

A: _____

Q: What note is it created on in the key of G major?

A: _____

Q: What key is the F# Mixolydian mode in?

A: _____

Q: What key is the D Mixolydian mode in?

A: _____

Chapter 5 Summary

In chapter five, we have learned about the 5th of the 7 modes. The Mixolydian mode. This is another major mode, but unique, in the other two due to the whole-step half-step formula and the note sequence this creates.

First, we learn that the Mixolydian mode is the 5th mode in the key of G major and located at the D note. This would be considered the D Mixolydian, and is also a major mode like the Ionian & Lydian.

Second, we learned the reason why the Mixolydian is major is because it has a natural 3rd. But, since the note formula is different from the other two major modes, the Ionian and Lydian, it has a different musical landscape.

Third, we learn how the notes of the Mixolydian mode span across the fretboard. This helps us to see that it stays that way no matter what key we choose to play it in, no matter if it's D Mixolydian or A Mixolydian.

Lastly, as with the other modes, and more to come, we look at guitar licks. These are phrases of notes within the mode that allow us to bring out its unique voice. Each mode has a unique voice, and the goal is to find it and bring it out.

Chapter 6 The Aeolian Mode

Lesson 26: What is the Aeolian mode?

Now we come to the 6th of the 7 modes, the Aeolian mode. This is another minor mode and the most popular of the 7 next to the Ionian.

The reason for this is the notes within it. Since it is a minor mode, we know it has a flat 3rd in it. But in addition to that, it also has a flat 6th and 7th. This makes it the natural minor mode.

Let's learn about this in more detail. If we take the G major scale and flatten the 3rd, 6th, and 7th notes, it becomes the G minor scale.

```
G major:  G  A  B  C  D  E  F#  G
          1  2  3  4  5  6  7   8

G minor:  G  A  Bb  C  D  Eb  F  G
          1  2  b3  4  5  b6  b7  8
```

By flattening these three notes, you create another scale. This scale is the Aeolian mode. Except for the key of G major, the Aeolian mode is located at the 6th note of the scale.

What is the 6th note of G major?

E is the sixth note of G major, and this is where the Aeolian mode is located. Let's take a look.

Key of G major: G A B C D E F# G
Ionian mode = 1 2 3 4 5 6 7 8

E Aeolian in G major: E F# G A B C D E
Aeolian mode =   1 2 b3 4 5 b6 b7 8

As you can see from above, the E Aeolian mode is the same as the G minor in the previous example. The difference is that the E minor is in the key of G major.

So we can conclude that the sixth of any major key is the Aeolian mode, and with the flat 3rd, 6th, and 7th, it becomes the relative minor of that key. This is because the Ionian and the Aeolian are made up of the same notes.

Remember, if you take the major scale and flatten the 3rd, 6th, and 7th, it creates the natural minor scale. But if you take the 6th note of the major scale and flatten the 3rd, 6th, and 7th notes, it becomes the relative minor to that major.

Every major key is going to have a relative minor and vice versa. Study this lesson to fully understand this concept.

Lesson 27: Characteristics of the Aeolian mode

The Aeolian mode has the characteristics of the natural minor. This is different than the other two minor modes, the Dorian and the Phrygian. It provides a traditional minor sound.

Like I showed you before, in the key of G major, the Aeolian mode is based on the sixth note. This makes it E minor. If we were in the key of C major, the same thing would apply.

```
C major:  C  D  E  F  G  A  B  C
          1  2  3  4  5  6  7  8
```

As we can see, the 6th note of this major scale is A, which means this is where the Aeolian mode would be located in this key.

```
A minor:  A  B  C   D  E  F   G   A
          1  2  b3  4  5  b6  b7  8
```

If you notice, these notes are the same as the C major. So even though it is the natural minor to A major, it becomes the relative to C major. This means you can move between the C major and the A minor and stay in harmony.

The whole-step and half-step formula for the Aeolian mode.

Aeolian mode: 1 2 b3 4 5 b6 b7 8
                   W H   W W H   W   W

Let's take a look at all 6 modes so far.

Ionian mode: 1 2 3 4 5 6 7   8 = major (natural 3rd)
              G A B C D E F# G

Dorian mode: 1 2 b3 4 5 6 b7 8 = minor (flat 3rd)
             A B C   D E F# G A

Phrygian mode: 1 b2 b3 4 5 b6 b7 8 = minor (flat 3rd)
                B C   D   E F# G   A   B

Lydian mode: 1 2 3 #4 5 6 7 8 = major (natural 3rd)
              C D E F# G A B C

Mixolydian mode: 1 2 3 4 5 6 b7 8 = major (natural 3rd)
                 D E F# G A B C   D

Aeolian mode: 1 2 b3 4 5 b6 b7 8 = minor (natural)
               E F# G A B C   D   E

As I stated before, master the difference in these modes that you have learned so far. Six down, one more to go.

Lesson 28: The Aeolian Mode in different keys

Now that we know a few things about the Aelian mode and its unique character, we can look at how it lays across the fretboard for a better understanding of it.

Once again, since we are in the key of G major (for easier learning), we will present it at the E position.

E Aeolian mode:

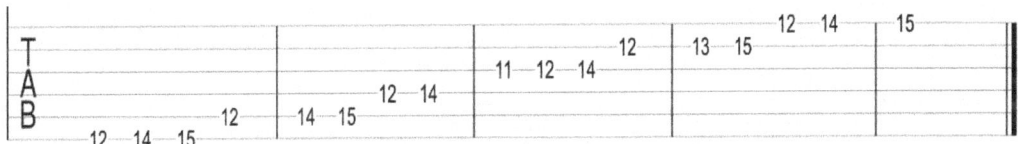

This mode will start on the 12th fret because that is where the E note is located. As it proceeds across the fretboard, it will develop a unique moody sound because of the notes within it. Which makes it a minor mode.

Remember, it is the whole-step, half-step formula that will determine the character of each mode. If it has a natural 3rd, it will sound happy; if it has a flat 3rd, it will sound sad.

Let's take a look at this mode in a few more keys.

58

F# Aeolian mode:

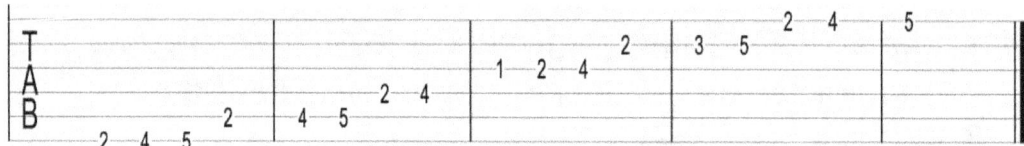

G Aeolian mode:

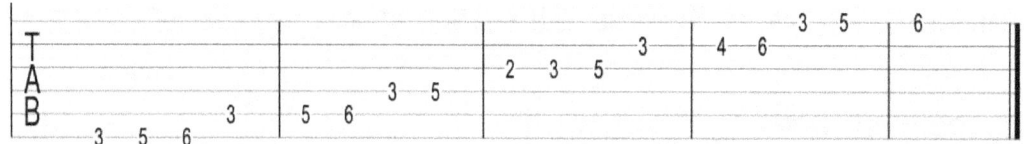

A Aeolian mode:

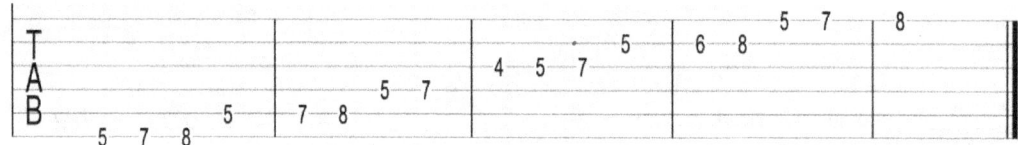

B Aeolian mode:

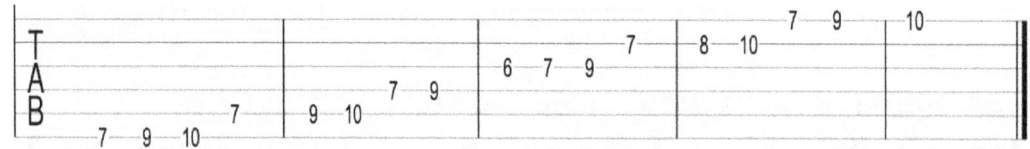

Like before, the pattern stays the same, and just the location changes. Make sure to master the mode, and then, as you play it in different locations, think about what key you are playing in.

Lesson 29: Aeolian mode guitar licks

Let's examine how we can bring the mode to life and make it sound musical. Like all the other modes, this is done with guitar licks. These will be presented in E Aeolian.

Guitar Lick #1:

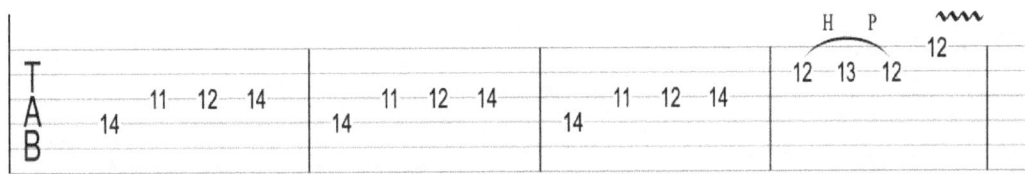

This example uses a repeated lick, a hammer-on pull-off, and ends with a vibrato on the 12th fret.

Guitar Lick #2:

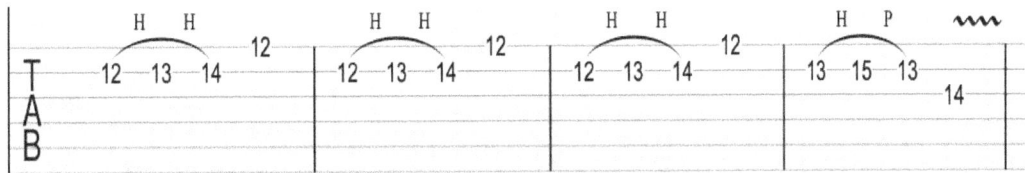

This example uses a repeated lick with a double hammer-on and ends with a hammer-on pull-off and vibrato.

Make sure to work at mastering the double hammer-on.

60

Guitar Lick #3:

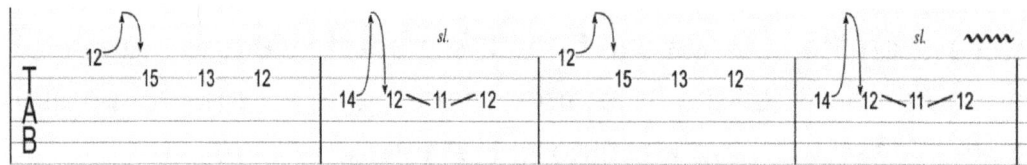

This example uses a bend release, a slide down and up, and it is repeated with a vibrato at the end.

Guitar Lick #4:

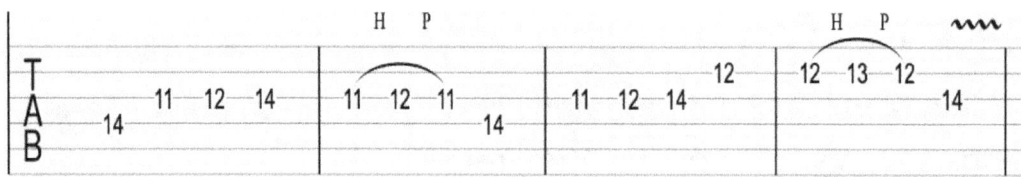

This example uses a repeated lick with a hammer-on pull-off and a vibrato at the end.

Guitar Lick #5:

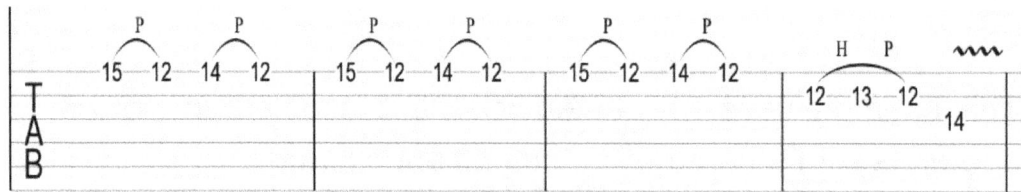

This example uses multiple pull-offs, a hammer-on pull-off and ends with a vibrato. Remember, vibrato is a great way to end a guitar lick or phrase.

Lesson 30: Chapter 6 Quiz

In this chapter, we have learned a lot about the Aeolian mode. Once again, a learning assessment is present to see how well you did and what you need to work on.

Q: What is the Aeolian mode?

A: _____

Q: Is the Aeolian mode major or minor?

A: _____

Q: What is the whole-step, half-step formula for the mode?

A: _____

Q: What makes this mode unique from the others?

A: _____

Q: What type of sound does the Aeolian mode convey?

A: _____

Q: What key is the F# Aeolian mode in?

A: _____

Q: What key is the B Aeolian mode in?

A: _____

Chapter 6 Summary

In chapter four, we have learned about the 6th of the 7 modes. The Aeolian mode. This is another minor mode, but it is unique in the fact that it is considered the natural minor, which gives it a different sound than the Dorian and Phrygian modes.

First, we learn that in the key of G major, the Aeolian mode is the 6th model located at the E note. This is the E Aeolian mode and has a different whole-step and half-step formula, which makes it unique.

Second, we learn that the Aeolian mode is minor because it has a flat 3rd, 6th, and 7th note in it. But, it is different than the Phrygian mode that incorporates the flat 2 note. Both are minor but have slightly different musical landscapes.

Third, we look at the way the Aeolian mode lays across the fretboard. Remember, just like the other modes, this pattern remains the same when played in different keys, but it changes from E Aeolian to F# Aeolian, B Aeolian, etc.

Study this chapter and make sure you fully understand the concepts I have taught you in it. They will help you to expand your knowledge of the 6 modes learned so far, and don't forget about the guitar licks within the mode as well.

Chapter 7 The Locrain Mode

Lesson 31: What is the Locrian mode?

Now we come to the 7th of the 7 modes, the Locrian mode. This mode is like the redheaded stepchild of the family. The reason is because of the note formula..

The Locrian mode is not a major or minor. It is a diminished mode. The reason for this is because it has a note that is different from the rest. It has a flat 5th note, and it is this flat 5th that gives it a unique sound.

In the key of G major, the Locrian mode will be in F#.

Key of G major: G A B C D E F# G
Ionian mode = 1 2 3 4 5 6 7 8

F# Locrian in G major: F# G A B C D E F#
Locrian mode = 1 b2 b3 4 b5 b6 b7 8

As you can see, the mode has all the flats as the other minor modes but adds the flat 5th. This flat 5th makes it diminished and gives it a dark and ominous sound. Perfect for creating that type of emotion.

Let's take a look at he difference between the minor modes and the Locrian.

The Dorian mode: 1 2 b3 4 5 6 b7 8

The Phrygian mode: 1 b2 b3 4 5 b6 b7 8

The Locrian mode: 1 b2 b3 4 b5 b6 b7 8

Notice that when you look at these minor modes side by side, they add flat notes to them. The Dorian mode has 2 flats, the Phrygian mode has 4 flats, and the Locrian has 5 flats.

What they all have in common is the flat 3rd note. As I said before, this is important to know because it is this flat 3rd note that creates a minor. No matter if it is a chord, scale, or a mode.

The thing about the Locrian mode is that because it has the flat 5th, it gives it a dissonant, almost unresolved sound, and the flat 2nd and 3rd create a tense and mysterious tone.

With this mode having the flattened 5th, it associates nicely with diminished chords, which are not usually presented in pop music but work well in darker styles.

Lesson 32: Characteristics of the Locrian mode

Since the Locrian mode has all the same notes as the Aeolian mode but adds the flat 2nd and flat 5th, it gives it a different type of moody aura. It is because of the whole-step and half-step note formula.

Let's take a look at the note formula.

F# Locrian mode: F# G A B C D E F#
                 1 b2 b3 4 b5 b6 b7 8
                 H W W H W W W

Since the Locrian mode has a flat 5th in it, you want to use that as a focal point. You want to create melodies that embrace tension and contrast to other note structures.

Practice improvising over chords and progressions that utilize notes within this mode. Remember, you take the notes from the mode above and create chords.

You then put those chords together to create a chord progression. By doing this, you create a certain type of mood or emotion, and since all the chords and melodies come from the mode, they will all fit in harmony with each other.

66

Lesson 33: The Locrian mode in different keys

Now that we know a few things about the Locrian mode, we want to learn how to play it across the fretboard. Since we're in the key of G major and it is the F# Locrian, I am going to present it in both positions for easier learning.

F# Locrian mode:

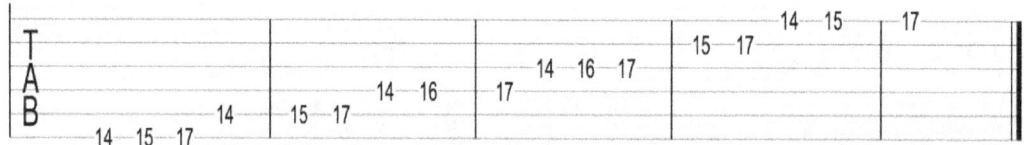

Here, the mode is presented at the F# on the 14th fret. This position can be a bit tricky to play if you're not used to it, so I will also present it at the lower end of the fretboard.

F# Locrian mode at the 2nd fret:

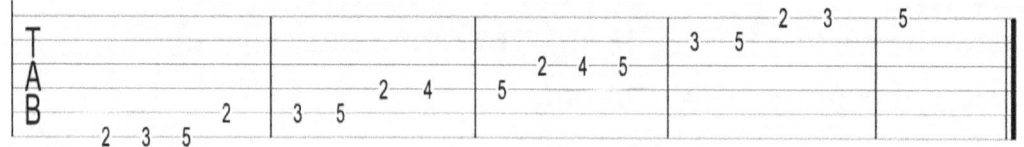

Here, the mode is presented at the F# on the 2nd fret in the lower position. I recommend you learn to play it and all other modes in both positions. This will help with ear training and fretboard knowledge.

G# Lorian mode:

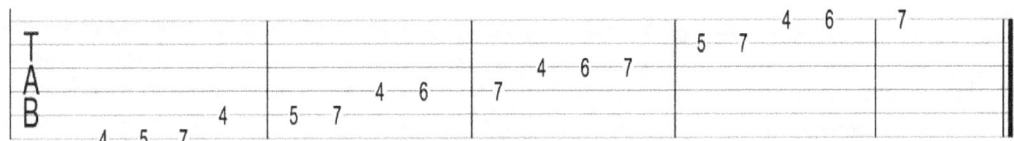

A# Locrian mode:

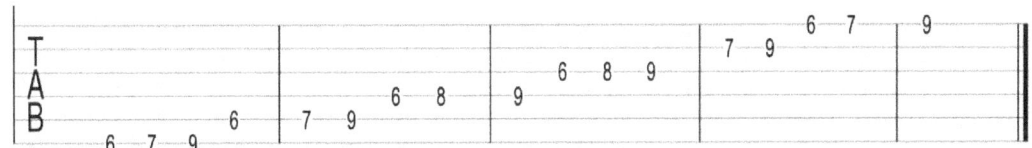

B Locrian mode:

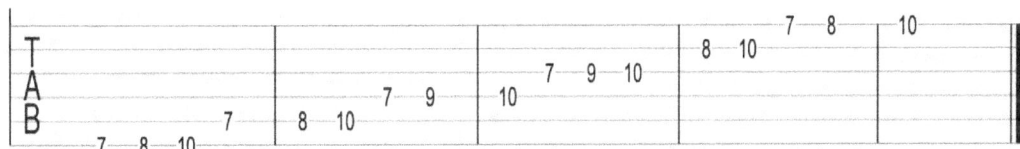

C# Locrian mode:

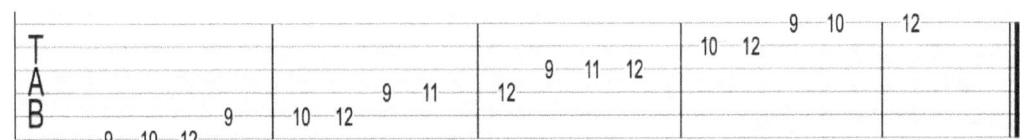

Some of these are in a sharp position (C#) because it is the 7th mode. This makes the mode in the major key in front of it.

Example: C# Locrian is in the key of D major.

68

Lesson 34: Locrian mode guitar licks

Here are some examples of guitar licks that can be created out of the Locrian mode. These will help us to master techniques such as bends, slides, etc, as well as bring the mode to life.

Once again, these will be presented in F# Locrian in the key of G major.

Guitar Lick #1:

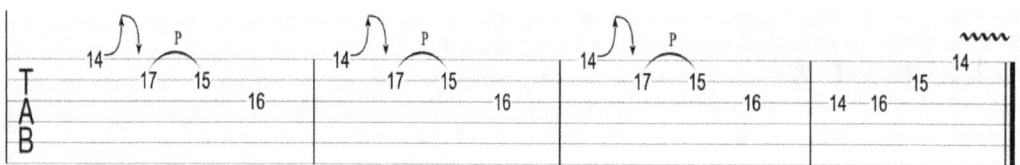

In this example, we use a bend release, a hammer-on, and a vibrato at the end.

Guitar Lick #2:

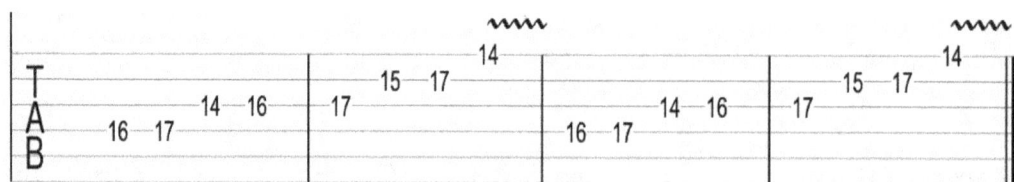

In this example, we have a simple run through the scale, with a vibrato at the end.

Remember to link the licks together to create phrasing.

Guitar Lick #3:

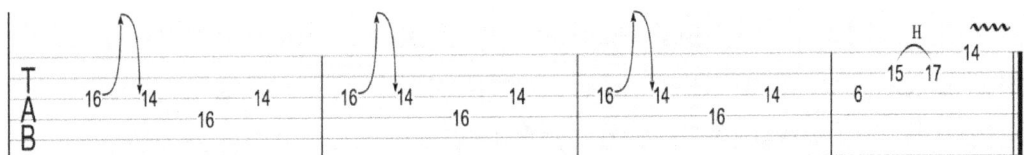

In this example, we use a repeated lick, a bend release, a hammer-on, and a vibrato.

Guitar Lick #4:

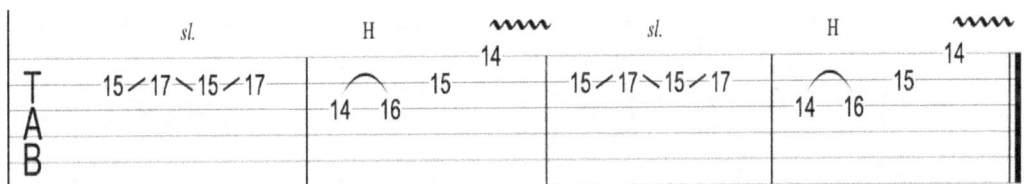

In this example, we use slides, hammer-on, vibrato, and a repeated lick.

Guitar Lick #5:

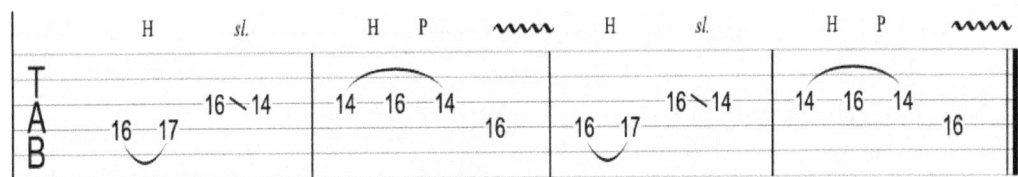

Here, we use a hammer-on, slide, hammer-on pull-off, vibrato, and a repeated lick.

Remember, practice these licks in the other keys presented.

Lesson 35: Chapter 7 Quiz

In this chapter, we have learned a lot about the Locrian mode, and once again, a learning assessment to see what you've learned and what still needs to be worked on is presented.

Q: What is the Locrian mode?

A: _____

Q: Is the Locrian mode major or minor?

A: _____

Q: What kind of sound does the Locrian mode produce?

A: _____

Q: What is the whole-step half-step formula?

A: _____

Q: What makes the Locrian mode unique?

A: _____

Q: What key is the B Locrian mode in?

A: _____

Q: Why key is the C Locrian mode in?

A: _____

Chapter 7 Summary

In chapter four, we learned about the last of the 7 modes. The Locrian mode. This is the 6th mode and allows you to explore unconventional sounds and emotions. This is because it has a kind of unresolved sound to it.

First, we learn that in the key of G major, the Locrian mode is the 6th mode located at the F# note. This is the F# Locrian mode, and because of its whole-step, half-step formula, it creates a sound of tension.

Second, we learn that the Locrian mode is not major or minor but a diminished mode. This is because it has a flat 5th note in it, and it is this flat note that gives it a unique character. Also makes it a bit odd from the others.

Third, we look at the way the Locrian mode lays across the fretboard. Like the other modes, this pattern remains the same when played in different locations. This is important to master as it makes it easier to play in multiple keys.

Lastly, we look at guitar licks that can be played within the Locrian mode. These simple melodies highlight the techniques that are commonly used in guitar playing.

72

Chapter 8: Chords Within The Modes

Lesson 36: Ionian and Dorian

In this chapter, we will learn about chords that can be created out of the modes. This lesson will look at the Ionian and Dorian modes.

Chords within the G Ionian mode: (Major)

G A B C D E F# G
1 2 3 4 5 6 7   8

G major = 1 3 5   GM6 = 1 3 5 6   GM7 = 1 3 5 7
       G B D   G B D E   G B D F#

Can you see how these chords can be created out of the notes of this mode?

We can also create, Gsus2 = 1 2 5 & Gsus4 = 1 4 5
                        G A D   G C D

Additional chords can be created as well, but these are the basics I would focus on for now. Since the Ionian mode is major, you can easily create major chords.

The Dorian mode works off of the same principle. But since the Dorian mode is minor, we will focus on these types of chords.

Remember, chords are created from the notes in the mode. That is why the 3rd note is so important. It distinguishes not only the type of tone you can get out of the mode but also the type of chords.

Chords within the A Dorian mode: (minor)

A B C D E F# G A
1 2 b3 4 5 6 b7 8

Am = 1 b3 5   Am6 = 1 b3 5 6   Am7 = 1 b3 5 b7
　　　A C E　　　　　　A C E D　　　　　　A C D G

Asus2 = 1 2 5   Asus4 1 4 5   Asus4 add6 1 2 5 6
　　　　　A B E　　　　　　A D E　　　　　　　　A B E F#

Your main chords will be the 1 3 5. In this case of the Dorian mode being minor, it will be 1 b3 5 because the 3rd note is flattened in this mode.

When you go beyond these notes, like in the sus4 add 6 chord, you extend the chord. Can you see how hundreds of chords can be created with this concept?

Lesson 37: Phrygian and Lydian

Now, we look at the Phrygian and Lydian modes. These will use the same concept as the Ionian and Dorian modes.

The Phrygian mode being minor, and the Lydian mode being major.

Chords within the B Phrygian mode: (minor)

```
B  C   D  E  F#  G  A  B
1  b2 b3  4  5   b6 b7 8
```

```
Bm = 1 b3 5    Bm6 = 1 b3  5  6     Bm7 = 1 b3 5 b7
     B  D  F#         B  D  F# G#          B  D  F# A
```

You can also create chords such as C major, D major, E minor, F# diminished, and, of course, G major.

All these can be created because of the triad concept learned earlier. C major = C E G. E minor = E G B. Can you see how these chords can be created because of the notes in the mode?

Since all the modes are made up of the same notes, all these chords can be created out of them in this particular key.

The Lydian mode is major, so we will focus on the major chords that can be created out of it. But like the Phrygian mode, additional chords can be created as well.

Chords within the C Lydian mode: (major)

```
C  D  E  F#  G  A  B  C
1  2  3  #4  5  6  7  8
```

```
C major = 1 3 5    CM6 = 1 3 5 6  CM7 1 3 5 7
          C E G            C E G A       C E G B
```

```
Csus2 = 1 2 5
        C D G
```

To create additional chords like in the last example with the Phrygian mode, you change the root of the chord. The root is the 1 of the chord. In this case, we are using the C note because we are in the C Lydian mode.

But if more chords are to be created out of the mode, we'd follow the same concept as before. If we use the G as the root, we can create G major. E as the root, we can create E minor.

Can you see how this concept works? This is why knowing the notes that make up a mode or key can be very beneficial.

Lesson 38: Mixolydian and Aeolian

Now, we look at chords that can be created from the Mixolydian mode as well as the Aeolian. Since we are in the key of G major, we will use D Mixolydian and E Aeolian.

Chords within the D Mixolydian mode: (major)

```
D  E  F#  G  A  B  C  D
1  2  3   4  5  6  b7 8
```

```
DM = 1  3  5   DM6 = 1 3 5 6  D7 = 1  3  5  b7
     D  F#  A        D F# A B        1 F#  A  C
```

```
Dsus2 = 1 2 5  Dsus4 1 4 5
        D E A        D G A
```

A major 7th chord will have a natural 7th in it, like the Ionian and Lydian. But the notes in this mode are configured in such a way that the C note becomes a flat 7th, and this allows us to create a different 7th chord, a dominant 7th chord.

Remember, it is all about how the notes line up in the mode that determines the chords that can be created out of it. It is this configuration of notes that gives each mode its character.

Now, we look at chords that come out of the Aeolian mode. Another minor mode. Once again, a minor mode or chord is going to have a flat 3rd note.

Chords within the E Aeolian mode: (minor)

```
E  F#  G  A  B  C  D  E
1   2  b3 4  5  b6 b7 8
```

```
Em = 1  b3  5    Emb6 1  b3  5  b6  Em7 = 1  b3  5  b7
     E  G   B          E  G   B  C         E  G   B  D
```

```
Esus2 = 1  2  5    Esus4 = 1  4  5    Esus4flat7 = 1  4  5  b7
        E  F# B             E  A  B                 E  A  B  D
```

As you can see from the examples above, you can create a lot of chords out of the mode if you just study the notes. This is a huge benefit for increasing your chord vocabulary.

In addition to these chords presented, you can also create the others once mentioned before. G major, D major, C minor, etc.

Why is this possible?

Because of all the notes that are in the modes.

Lesson 39: Locrian & Progressions

Now we come to the Locrian mode. The one that is the most unique.

Why?

It has the flat 5th note and is the only one of the 7 modes that does. Being that it has the flat 3rd and flat 5th, it makes it a diminished mode.

Chords within the F# Locrian mode: (diminished)

```
F#  G   A   B   C    D   E   F#
1   b2  b3  4   b5   b6  b7  8
```

```
F#dim = 1  b3 b5   F#mb5 = 1  b3 b5  b7   GM = 1  3  5
        F#  A  C            F# A  C   E         G  B D
```

As you can see, if we change the root note to G, we can create the G major chord. The same thing goes for all the other notes.

```
Am = 1  b3  5   Bm = 1  b3 5   CM = 1 3 5   DM = 1  3  5
      A   C   E        B  D F#        C E G        D F# A
```

Remember, if you study the notes in any key, you'll be able to create chords and melodies to create musical landscapes.

Chord progressions

Once you learn what chords you can create out of the modes, you can then work at putting them together to create chord progressions.

Chord progressions are based on the key that they come out of and make up the foundation of most songs.

Here are a few simple progressions to get started wth. Once you get them down, try using other chords in their place.

Chord progression #1:

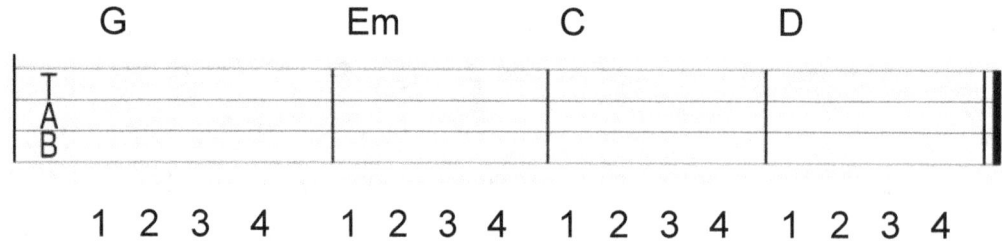

This is a very common chord progression. Either strum or arpeggiate the chords to hear how they sound.

Try out the guitar licks you learned and see how they sound over this progression.

Chord progression #2:

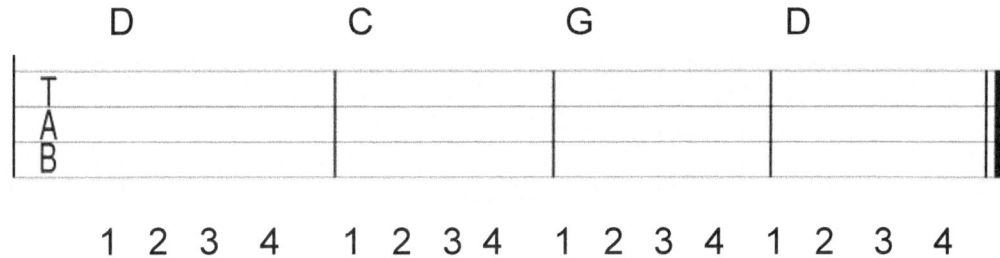

This progression starts with the D major chord and goes through a similar chord progression.

Chord progression #3:

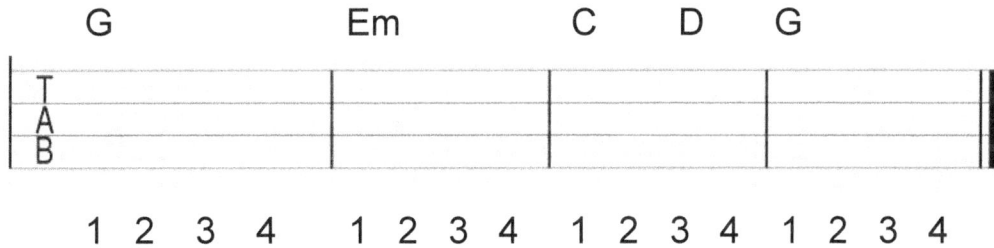

This example is similar to the first one, except we play two chords within the third measure. Here, each chord will play for only 2 beats instead of 4. Listen to how this changes the rhythm.

These are just a few examples to start with. Take these ideas and expand on them. Use different chords and change the Timing.

82

Here are a few blank measures for you to create chord
progressions of your own. Use the chords that you have
learned and see how they sound.

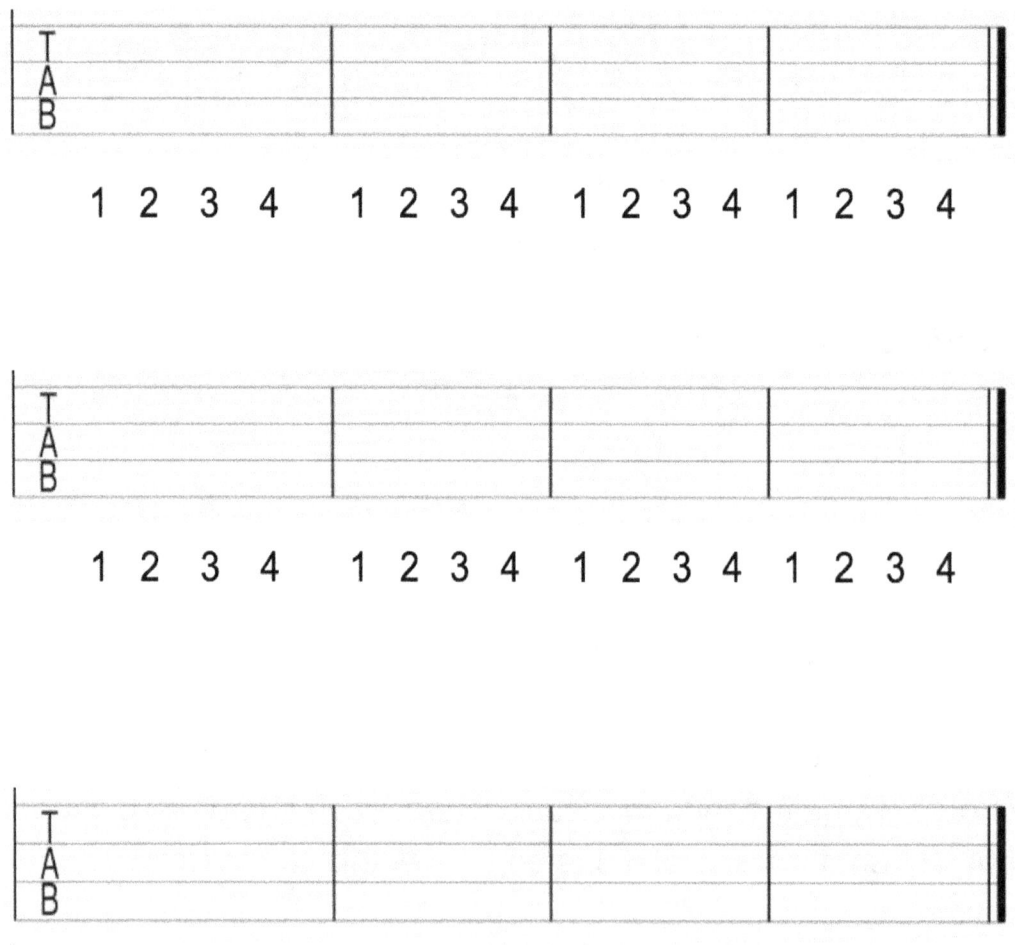

Lesson 40: Chapter 8 Quiz

Once again, we have a simple assessment exercise (or quiz) to make sure you know the material in this chapter.

Q: What chords are within the Ionian mode?

A: _____

Q: What chords are within the Dorian mode?

A: _____

Q: What chords are within the Phrygian mode?

A: _____

Q: What chords are within the Lydian mode?

A: _____

Q: What chords are within the Mixolydian mode?

A: _____

Q: What chords are within the Aeolian mode?

A: _____

Q: What chords are within the Locrian mode?

A: _____

Review this chapter well, as it will enhance your musicality.

Chapter 8 Summary

In this chapter, we have learned a few chords that can be created out of the 7 modes, as well as a few basic chord progressions to get started.

With each mode offering a specific set of note intervals, we can create harmonically rich compositions of different variations.

First, we look at chords that can be formed out of the Ionian mode and the Dorian mode. The Ionian being major and the Dorian being minor, it is good to focus on these types of chords,

Second, we look at chords that can be formed from the Phrygian and Lydian modes. Phrygian major.

Third, we look at the Mixolydian mode and the Aeolian mode. These create a nice assortment of chords as well. With the Mixolydian being major and the Aeolan being minor.

Fourth, we look at chords within the Locrian mode and basic chord progressions that can be formed for better rhythm and lead guitar playing.

Each mode has a unique sound quality that you want to explore to create versatile musical compositions.

Remember,

The **Ionain mode** is <u>major</u> 1 2 3 4 5 6 7 8

The **Dorian mode** is <u>minor</u> 1 2 b3 4 5 6 b7 8

The **Phrygian mode** is <u>minor</u> 1 b2 b3 4 5 b6 b7 8

The **Lydian mode** is <u>major</u> 1 2 3 #4 5 6 7 8

The **Mixolydian mode** is <u>major</u> 1 2 3 4 5 6 b7 8

The **Aeolian mode** is <u>minor</u> 1 2 b3 4 5 b6 b7 8

The **Locrian mode** is <u>diminished</u> 1 b2 b3 4 b5 b6 b7 8

Study these note intervals for a better understanding of each mode and how they differ slightly from each other. Notice how their difference in note intervals allows them to stay in harmony with the key they come out of.

86

Guitar Modes Conclusion

If you've made it this far, I congratulate you on your accomplishments and say, "Thank you for your purchase of this book and your time learning to play what I have taught". You seem like the kind of student that I'd love to teach in person.

The Ionian mode has a certain characteristic due to its whole-step and half-step note sequence. Remember, this mode has a nice, bright, uplifting sound quality, and it is great for this type of emotion.

The Dorian mode is minor and known for its sad, moody tone quality. With its flat 3rd and flat 7th, it has a soft minor quality with a bluesy element. Be sure to master this mode across the fretboard and use it for this type of emotion.

The Phrygian mode is another minor, but wth a different sound quality. The reason for this is that it has two more flat notes. The flat 2nd and 6th, and because of these intervals, it provides a dark, exotic sound. Great for this type of emotion.

The Lydian mode is major but different from the Ionian because of its unique note structure. In addition to having a natural 3rd, it also has a sharp 4th. It is this note interval that gives this mode a sound of wonder and exploration.

The Mixolydian mode is another major, but different from the Lydian and Ionian in the fact that it has a natural 3rd, but also a flat 7th note. This interval note structure gives it a dominant sound quality, and it is great for conveying this emotion.

The Aeolian mode is minor and has the flat 3rd, 6th, and 7th notes. What makes it unique from the Dorian and Phrygian modes is that it creates the natural minor sound. This also makes it relative to the Ionian mode.

The Locrian mode is not major or minor but diminished because it has both the flat 3rd and flat 5th. This gives it a very dark, ominous tone quality that seems unresolved and is great for conveying this type of emotion.

Remember these qualities of each mode and explore them in your compositions. If you have any questions, feel free to contact me at my website below, and I will be happy to help. My way of saying thanks for purchasing my book.

Visit my website at DwaynesGuitarLessons.com.

To all your success,

Sincerely, Dwayne Jenkins
copyright © 2025

Other Books From Tritone Publishing

Learn To Play Rhythm Guitar:

This book is designed for anyone who wants to learn to play rhythm guitar or enhance their rhythm guitar playing skills. Loaded with pictures, diagrams, and notation for productive study.

Playing rhythm guitar is a great way to master chords, timing, finger strength, fretboard knowledge, and music theory. All in a simple step-by-step method that anyone can learn from.

How To Play Guitar Solos:

A method book tailored for beginners. If you can play rhythm guitar and want to learn lead guitar, this book is for you. It's packed with everything you need to get started.

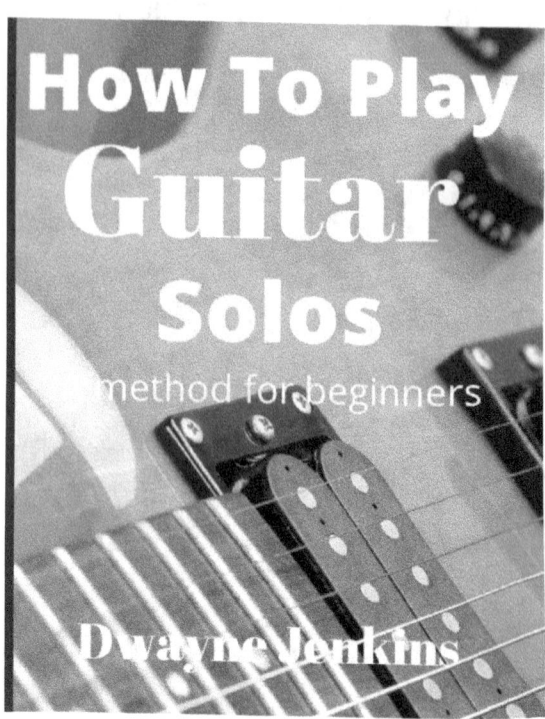

A comprehensive training course with pictures, diagrams, and notation for quick study. With a simple step-by-step method that will have you playing guitar solos in no time. Even if you have no previous knowledge of music.

Learn Guitar Chord Theory:

Have you ever looked at notation and wondered what a Cadd9 chord is? Or possibly a Gsus4? If you have, this book will explain what it is, how to create it, and how to use it.

Learn Guitar Chord Theory is a comprehensive study guide on the inner workings of guitar chords. Take the time to develop an extended chord vocabulary and mix it with a full understanding of how they work.

All books are authored by Dwayne Jenkins, published by Tritone Publishing, and can be found worldwide.

Digital formats of all titles are also available for quicker learning. Just download them onto your computer and start learning right away.

Self-study is a great way to learn as it allows you to not only go at your own pace but also develop the skills of self-discipline and time management. Which can benefit you in other areas of your life.

Also, check out Dwayne's Guitar Lessons video channel on YouTube. These are free lessons that cover a wide variety of topics related to playing guitar.

Whether you are working on rhythm, lead, theory, or guitar maintenance, it is all here in these lessons. Which are available 24 hours a day, 7 days a week, 365 days a year.

And if more help is needed, Dwayne also offers one-on-one private coaching. Which can be found on his website.

https:dwaynesguitarlessons.com

Best of luck, and have fun. Tritone Publishing © 2025

About the Author

Dwayne Jenkins is a professional guitar teacher, an accomplished musician, and an entrepreneur. He has been learning, playing, and teaching guitar lessons throughout Denver, CO, for over two decades.

He is now bringing his special training skills and methodology that have been honed and hand-crafted throughout the years on how to play to students around the world.

Dwayne has a unique, exciting approach that gets students of all ages and skill levels enjoying the fun of playing guitar and ukulele. His enthusiasm and love for teaching shine through every lesson that he creates.

His lessons are designed to enhance your ability to progress. No matter your reason for learning, there will always be something in Dwayne's books and products to help you achieve your dreams.

So if you're a student looking to start or a student looking to further your education, be sure to get involved with Dwayne's guitar lessons and learn what so many people have already discovered: why learning to play the guitar or ukulele is one of the greatest things you can do for yourself.

94

What Students Are Saying About Dwayne's Guitar Lessons

"Dwayne, thank you so much for everything you have taught me and done for me. You are an amazing guitarist and wonderful teacher". BJ

"Dwayne, it has been a true pleasure to have you at our house each week! Ken & Trevor have learned so much through you and your teachings. Thank you!" Lisa

"Dwayne, thank you for being a great teacher and teaching me many great songs. This is a skill that will last me a lifetime." Danielle

"Dwayne, we want you to know we are honored to have you at the studio. We appreciate all that you do and are grateful that we can leave you in charge." Angie & Wilson M.E.C.

"Dwayne, we are so glad you are our Teacher. It's been three years already, can you believe it? Thank you again. You're the best!" Chelsey & Lucas.

"Dwayne, we are so glad that you are in our lives. Chelsey & Lucas enjoy their time with you and look up to you. Looking forward to another great year!" Love and best wishes, Ken & Sue.

"Dwayne, thank you so much for being not only an awesome guitar teacher but an awesome friend as well," Kayla.

"Dwayne, thank you so much for all the years of doing lessons. You have been very patient with my progress, helped me to build confidence in myself, and inspired me to follow my dreams. And in doing so, you have become a great friend." Jake.

"Dwayne, thank you for teaching Nick guitar so well. He loves it and is getting quite good fast. I'm amazed!" Jane.

"Dwayne, thank you so much for teaching me every Saturday and not only teaching me guitar but also about life and helping me with setting my goals. You are a great teacher, mentor, and the best friend ever." Carson.

"There is not another person I would want to be teaching me a guitar! His 1 on 1 teaching makes learning guitar very personal & exhilarating. He teaches at your pace and takes pride in what YOU want to learn. The best part is that if Dwayne doesn't know a song a student wants to play, he takes time out of the week to learn it. His teaching comes to life in my performance and has progressed over the last 8 years. Words cannot describe how amazing a teacher, rockstar, and true friend Dwayne has become to me." Dominic.